THE ESSENCE OF

# EXPERT SYSTEMS

## THE ESSENCE OF COMPUTING SERIES

**Published Titles**

The Essence of Artificial Intelligence
The Essence of Compilers
The Essence of Computing Projects – A Student's Guide
The Essence of Databases
The Essence of Discrete Mathematics
The Essence of Human–Computer Interaction
The Essence of Java Programming
The Essence of Logic
The Essence of Neural Networks
The Essence of Professional Issues in Computing
The Essence of Program Design
The Essence of Programming Using C++
The Essence of Structured Systems Analysis Techniques

**Forthcoming Titles**

The Essence of Distributed Systems
The Essence of Information Technology

# THE ESSENCE OF

# EXPERT SYSTEMS

**Keith Darlington**
South Bank University

*An imprint of* Pearson Education

Harlow, England · London · New York · Reading, Massachusetts · San Francisco
Toronto · Don Mills, Ontario · Sydney · Tokyo · Singapore · Hong Kong · Seoul
Taipei · Cape Town · Madrid · Mexico City · Amsterdam · Munich · Paris · Milan

**Pearson Education Limited**
Edinburgh Gate
Harlow
Essex, CM20 2JE
England

and Associated Companies throughout the world

*Visit us on the World Wide Web at:*
http://www.pearsoneduc.com



First published 2000

Typeset in Times 10/12 by 30

Printed an bound in Great Britain by Biddles Ltd, *www.biddles.co.uk*

Library of Congress Cataloging-in-Publication Data

A catalog record for this book is available from the Library of Congress

British Library Cataloguing in Publication Data

A catalogue record for this book is available from the British Library

ISBN 0-13-022774-9

10 9 8 7 6 5 4 3 2
05 04 03 02 01

To Janice

# Contents

# Series preface

As the consulting editor for the Essence of Computing series it is my role to encourage the production of well-focused, high-quality textbooks at prices that students can afford. Since most computing courses are modular in structure, we aim to produce books that will cover the essential material for a typical module.

I want to maintain a consistent style for the series so that whenever you pick up an Essence book you know what to expect. For example, each book contains important features such as end of chapter summaries and exercises, and a glossary of terms, if appropriate. Of course, the quality of the series depends crucially on the skills of its authors, and all the books are written by lecturers who have honed their material in the classroom. Each book in the series takes a pragmatic approach and emphasises practical examples and case studies.

Our aim is that each book will become essential reading material for students attending core modules in computing. However, we expect students to want to go beyond the Essence books, and so all books contain guidance on further reading and related work.

The study of expert systems has now matured, and we understand how to use such systems. This book provides an excellent pragmatic introduction to the field of expert systems, suitable for an advanced undergraduate or postgraduate taught module. It explains what expert systems can be used for, compares different types of system, and gives many examples of expert systems that have successfully been used in practice. It also clearly presents the underlying theory needed to understand the different aspects of expert system construction and use.

Computing is constantly evolving, and so the teaching of the subject also has to change. Therefore the series has to be dynamic, responding to new trends in computing and extending into new areas of interest. We need feedback from our readers to guide us – are we hitting the target? Are there "hot" topics that we have not yet covered ? Feedback is always welcome, but most of all I hope you find this book useful!

**Ray Welland**
*Department of Computing Science*
*University of Glasgow*
(e-mail: ray@dcs.gla.ac.uk)

# Preface

The aim of this book is to provide a complete course text for computing students studying a first course unit in expert systems. The material in this book is based on single-semester undergraduate courses held for students at the South Bank University, London.

There is a need for a self-contained text that covers the fundamentals of expert systems and reflects the structure of the one-semester unit now common in many undergraduate courses. The structure of this book needs to combine an understanding of the theoretical principles and techniques with the development of practical skills that are required to build expert systems. This is best achieved by gaining practical experience with appropriate software tools. Amongst the most commonly used tools for building expert systems are "expert system shells". Thus, many of the techniques and concepts described in the early chapters are illustrated using shells, and one of the later chapters is devoted entirely to shells. Many of the techniques of expert systems are taught using shells where appropriate.

There is also a need to provide the reader with an understanding of the range of skills that are necessary to build an expert system. These skills range from the capturing of the "human expertise" through to the system design, programming, implementation testing and maintenance of the final system.

The text is structured according to the Prentice Hall Essence series. That is, a textbook that contains about 12 chapters of 200 pages in total. Each chapter begins with a set of objectives to enable readers to know in advance what they will be expected to understand when they have finished reading the chapter. Each chapter also contains a number of questions interspersed throughout the text that enable readers to check their understanding of the material covered. These questions are intended to encourage a reflective approach to learning this subject, so the answers should take no more than a few minutes. Each chapter ends (apart from Chapter 1) with a set of further exercises. Some of these exercises encourage the reader to check on his or her factual knowledge; others test a broader understanding of the topic.

The early chapters begin with the history and potential benefits of expert systems, and are followed by an overview of the concepts of expert systems. This section also examines the different problems to which expert systems can be applied and considers different ways to represent these problems as well as looking at the methods of inference that can be applied to the problems. The expert system development life-cycle from knowledge acquisition, through design, to implementation, testing and maintenance is also included in this section.

Chapters 9 and 10 provide the reader with an insight into the design and implementation of a rule-based expert system using the expert system shell called VP-Expert. Practical exercises are included to consolidate the material learned. Some of the questions in these exercises are based on VP-Expert. However, the material in this chapter has been written in such a way that it will not be necessary for the reader to have access to this shell. VP-Expert is fairly easy to learn, and to use, and expert systems can be built rapidly using this shell. Moreover, this shell is used extensively in higher education in the UK.

# Acknowledgements

I would like to thank my colleagues at South Bank University for their general support and comments: in particular, Dr Fintan Culwin for his invaluable comments and encouragement throughout the project, and Dr Val Flynn, who also provided useful comments and support.

Special thanks also go to Dr Ray Welland of the University of Glasgow for the time and support he gave throughout the project, and Nicky McGirr, Ellen Lewis and Julie Knight at Pearson Education for their invaluable help and advice.

Finally, but most importantly, thanks to Rhiannon, Katie, Amy and Janice for putting up with me during those many hours spent tapping away at the keyboard.

**Keith Darlington**
*May 1999*

CHAPTER 1

# *AI and expert systems: a brief history*

**Objectives**

In this chapter you will learn:

- to appreciate the link between AI and expert systems;
- to understand the historical development of KBS and likely directions for the future;
- to appreciate the benefits arising from the use of KBS in business;
- to recognise KBS as decision support systems;
- to compare and contrast KBS and decision support systems.

## 1.1 Introduction

This book is about expert systems or knowledge-based systems (KBS) as they are also known. Such systems owe their origin to another field of study called artificial intelligence (AI). The ideas of AI began to emerge as a separate field of study in the 1940s. Some 50 years on much has happened to AI – there have been many success stories and many perceived failures. This chapter begins with a brief history of AI and KBS so that the reader can gain a better appreciation of the likely future directions of this controversial branch of computer science.

## 1.2 The beginnings of AI

Research in AI began during the 1940s; it was during this time that the first generation of computers appeared in research institutes. The foundations of machine logic were based on mathematics pioneered by the work of Kurt Godel, Alonzo Church and Alun Turing, and Whitehead and Russell (1913) helped to produce formalised methods in logical reasoning. Their principal research focused on propositional and predicate calculus. These logic formalisms have since played a significant part in AI systems. Turing (1950) developed the Turing machine, which demonstrated that a simple number processor could manipulate symbols as well as numbers. He later became better known for the so called *Turing Test*, used for comparing machine and human intelligence.

However, it was not until 1956 that John Mcarthy first used the term "artificial intelligence" during a conference held at Dartmouth College in the USA. Several scientists who were working in this newly emerging field of study attended the conference. Their enthusiasm for this new discipline was such that they predicted that in 25 years we would all be involved in recreational activities, while computers would be doing all the work.

Twenty-five years later, as is now known, it is clear that such predictions were over optimistic. AI did not fulfil expectations. The reason for this lay in the assumptions made by these scientists at that time. It was assumed that problems that were deemed to require high intelligence by a human being, such as advanced mathematical problems, would equally require much intelligence by a machine. Computers, even at this time, were very successful at such problems.

One of the most significant AI programs of the period was the Logic Theorist by Newell, Shaw and Simon (1963). This program was able to prove 38 of the 52 theorems of Whitehead and Russell's (1913) *Principia Mathematica*. Other programs displaying high mathematical competence followed. Some of these programs displayed competence on a par with final-year undergraduate mathematics students. In retrospect, this may not be such a surprise when it is considered that the language of the computer is Boolean logic. However, the view taken at the time was that programs empowered with smart reasoning techniques could be generalised beyond the domain of mathematical problems to other spheres of human activity. It seemed appropriate, to the AI community of the time, to extend these classes of problems beyond the mathematics sphere into real-world problems by focusing on general problem-solving techniques.

## 1.3 General problem-solving AI programs

In the late 1950s, AI scientists tried to emulate the "thinking processes" underlying human reasoning by finding general methods for solving broad classes of problems. One such project, developed by Newell and Simon (1976), was known as the general problem solver algorithm or GPS. A specific problem would be described to GPS in terms of an existing, initial situation and a goal situation. The knowledge system contained operators that would determine how the system could move from one state to the next, towards a goal state. For example, in a game of chess, the operators are the rules that enable the various pieces to move on the board from one state to the other. Such problems are characterised by a state space search (SSS). The SSS paradigm is one of the major AI paradigms in use today and will be discussed in more detail in Chapter 2.

GPS was successful in diverse problem-solving areas such as theorem proving, integral calculus and a variety of logic puzzles. Despite these successes the general strategy failed for two reasons: first, search spaces grow very large as problems become more general, precipitating the so-called combinatorics explosion. The second was the problem of representation, for while problem solver programs described and represented mathematical problems relatively easily, it turned out to be incredibly difficult to represent everyday life problems. Consequently, in the 1960s, AI research moved towards methods for improving search algorithms and techniques for representing knowledge. Chapter 2 examines search algorithms in more detail while Chapter 3 is devoted entirely to "knowledge representation."

## 1.4 The birth of KBS

One of the shortcomings of the general problem-solving approach was that as the size of the problem increased, so the ensuing search space grew exponentially. Only by making such programs less general, and concentrating on the specific knowledge pertaining to the problem, could such search spaces be reduced. Thus a new thrust of research emerged in the 1970s that attempted, as Waterman (1986) states, "To make a program intelligent, provide it with lots of high-quality, specific knowledge about some problem area." Lenat and Guha (1991) were later to call this the *knowledge principle*. They state this as follows: "If a program is to perform a complex task well it must know a great deal about the world in which it operates. In the absence of knowledge, all you have left is search and reasoning, and that isn't enough."

From the first crop of KBS that emerged, there was an emphasis on real-life domains such as diagnosing infectious diseases or predicting mineral deposits in various geographic regions of the world. This was an era of experimentation on real-life problems to see if the ideas were achievable in practice. The DENDRAL system was the first such system to be built. Work commenced on this system in 1965 under the direction of Edward Feigenbaum (1982). The system was used to assess the chemical structures of unknown molecules. Because such systems were used to solve problems that would otherwise require the services of an expert, they became known as expert systems. They have also come to be known as knowledge-based systems or knowledge systems, because they are systems that possess knowledge about some particular domain. Other experimental research-based expert systems are described in Table 1.1.

Table 1.1 *Some experimental expert systems*

| *Name* | *Place of origin* | *Year* | *Description of domain* |
|---|---|---|---|
| DENDRAL | Stanford University, USA | 1965 | Discovers molecular structures given only information on the constituents and mass spectral data |
| MACSYMA | MIT, USA | 1968 | A large interactive program that solves several types of mathematical problem, including integral calculus |
| PROSPECTOR | Stanford Research Institute | 1974 | Assists geologists in mineral exploration. Can also predict likelihood of detecting geological finds in certain areas |
| MYCIN | Stanford University, USA Shortliffe | 1976 | A medical system originally developed to assist doctors in the selection of antibiotics for severe infections |
| XCON | DEC | 1980 | Configures DEC VAX mainframe computers |

## 1.5 The emergence of commercial expert systems

Many of the expert systems that were built in the 1970s were experimental and confined mainly to academic research. It was not until the 1980s that they started to make the transition from research laboratory to commercial systems. The XCON system (McDermott 1982) was amongst the first. DEC built this in the early 1980s. It is the epitome of a successful expert system, being reputed to have saved enormous sums of money for the company and produced a return on investment in a very short time. XCON has a customer configuration accuracy of 98% compared with 70% for humans, and does the job in a fraction of the time taken by a human being to complete. The success of XCON triggered the beginning of a commercial boom for expert systems, and by the late 1980s companies large and small were jumping on the bandwagon to explore the potential of expert systems.

### *Japanese and US interest in expert systems*

In Japan, a massive 10 year fifth-generation project began in 1982. The aim of this project was to develop the so-called fifth-generation computers based on AI and parallel processing. The project was very extensive, covering themes such as intelligent software environments, parallel processing, hardware, and much more. The USA also took a great deal of interest in the emerging technology with the Advanced Research Projects Agency (ARPA) funding two major programmes in AI. These events helped to trigger much of the commercial interest in AI and expert systems at that time.

### *UK and European interest in AI and expert systems*

The UK also has a long tradition in computer science and AI. The "Turing Test" (Turing 1950) has been a litmus test for machine intelligence for many years. The Lighthill Report, however (Lighthill 1972), almost destroyed AI research in the UK. It condemned AI as a theoretical toy and concluded that most AI applications had so much variety that computers would be caught in a "combinatorial explosion." Much research in AI was, at the time, dedicated to developing search strategies to help combat this combinatorics explosion. Nevertheless, the influence of the report virtually terminated support for AI research in the UK in the 1970s.

AI was given a new lease of life in the UK following the extensive interest in AI by the Japanese fifth-generation project. This was the catalyst for the 5 year Alvey project that began in the UK in 1984, which recommended a major investment in intelligent knowledge-based systems (IKBS). IKBS were chosen to avoid the term AI following the adverse publicity it received owing to the Lighthill Report. The project was a collaboration between the Department of Trade and Industry (DTI), UK industry and academia. Proposals were unlikely to get funding unless they demonstrated industrial and academic co-operation. The project received some £350 million from the DTI in 1984 and several UK companies including GEC, ICL, Logica, BA, Rolls-Royce, Royal Assurance, and many more collaborators. Over 200 demonstrator projects were developed of which at least half were considered to be successful. One example of such demonstrator systems was Aires, a project that involved insurance companies in fire risk assessment. A system for the Department of Health and Social Security (DHSS) (Bramer 1986) was another.

The economic integration that took place in Europe during the 1980s also paved the way for European initiatives in IT projects. The most notable was ESPRIT (European Strategic Programme for Research in Information Technology) project. AI and KBS were a significant theme in the ESPRIT programme.

## 1.6 AI into the twenty-first century

There are several projects attracting the attention of the AI community at present. The most notable is the CYC project (Lenat and Guha 1991) which started in 1984. CYC is taken from the word EN<u>CYC</u>LOPAEDIA because it attempts to store a vast amount of real-world knowledge. The project is based at the Microelectronics and Computer Technology Corporation (MCC) in Austin, Texas, and is one of the most ambitious projects ever undertaken in AI. The project leader and founder, Doug Lenat, was quoted as saying: "The motive behind CYC is that the first generation of expert systems lack common sense." This has caused them to be "brittle." This meant that many first-generation expert systems performed very well but only when confined to the narrow boundaries of the domain knowledge used by the systems. These systems would be unable to respond sensibly to broader real-world common-sense knowledge that human experts frequently use because they did not have any. As an example of this problem, consider the following expert system dialogue on skin disease diagnosis with a patient who is a 1969 Chevrolet car.

| | |
|---|---|
| *Program:* | Are there any spots on the body? |
| *User:* | Yes. |
| *Program:* | What colour spots? |
| *User:* | Reddish brown. |
| *Program:* | Are there more spots on the trunk than elsewhere? |
| *User:* | No. |
| *Program:* | The patient has measles. |

The above example demonstrates that expert systems can produce bizarre output when confronted with unexpected situations. Human experts overcome this problem of brittleness by drawing upon general or common-sense knowledge.

CYC is an attempt to encode the hundreds and thousands of facts and heuristics that comprise human common-sense knowledge. Lenat and Guha (1991) believe that the absence of common sense is important because of what they call the breadth hypothesis. This states: "To behave intelligently in unexpected situations, an agent must be capable of falling back on increasingly general knowledge and analogizing to specific but far flung knowledge." Lenat and Feigenbaum support this belief with substantial empirical evidence.

Table 1.2 shows a range of some highly successful commercial expert systems developed and used since 1990.

Expert systems have brought considerable benefits to organisations over the last 15 years. Some generic success areas are listed below and are described in more detail in Chapter 12.

- Diagnosis (e.g. the MYCIN system in Table 1.1).
- Design (e.g. NSPP in Table 1.2).
- Planning (e.g. the DART system in Table 1.2).
- Configuration (e.g. the XCON system described in Section 1.5).
- Scheduling (e.g. GPSS in Table 1.2).

## 1.7 Human expertise compared with expert systems

Despite the successes, there have been many examples of expert system failures. The appropriateness of using expert systems for a particular project will be discussed in Chapter 11. However, the general advantages and disadvantages of expert systems and human expertise can be summarised as follows.

Table 1.2 *Expert systems developed since 1990*

| *Name* | *Developer* | *Year of completion* | *Description* |
|---|---|---|---|
| GPSS (Ground Processing Scheduled System) | NASA, USA | 1993 | A scheduling expert system. Schedules operations for the recycling of Space Shuttle flights from one flight to the next |
| NSSP | Nippon Steel, Japan | 1992 | A design expert system. Used for designing customer steel requirements. Uses case-based reasoning |
| FRAUDWATCH | Touche Ross, UK | 1992 | A monitoring expert system. Used by Barclays Bank to detect fraud in use of credit cards |
| DART | DARPA, USA | 1990 | A planning expert system. Used for logistics planning during the Gulf War |
| LINKMAN | Blue Circle plc, UK | 1991 | A process control expert system. Used for controlling energy consumption in cement production |

### *Computer advantages*

- Human expertise is perishable. For example, humans may change jobs, they can become ill, and so on. Computer expertise, on the other hand, is permanent.
- Human expertise is not always consistent. Human experts can have "off-days", busy schedules, and so on, all of which could adversely affect their normal performance. Computers are always consistent, and given identical conditions they will always give the same advice.
- Human expertise is difficult to transfer: a human being cannot be in two places at the same time. Computer expertise is relatively easy to transfer. For example, an expert system running on a PC could be copied to another PC at a different site, or downloaded onto a network of PCs, or even downloaded from the Internet.
- Human expertise is expensive. Employee salaries are far greater than the cost of PC hardware and software. Expert systems, even taking into account development costs, are much more affordable.

### *Human advantages*

- Humans are creative, often inspired; computers are uninspired.
- Humans are flexible, and easily adapt or integrate their expertise with other domain knowledge; computers are not very flexible in this respect.
- Humans possess common sense. Expert systems cannot apply knowledge to a problem beyond the domain knowledge, and thus have a narrow focus of the problem.
- Expert system programs have capabilities for learning that transcend those available in a conventional program. However, such capabilities are still very primitive compared with human learning.

## 1.8 Benefits of expert systems

Benefits of expert systems can be accrued both to the organisation and to the individual working within the organisation.

### *Organisational advantages*

- *Knowledge retention.* The knowledge is permanent, unlike that of a human expert, who may switch employment, retire, etc.
- *Knowledge distribution.* The knowledge can be distributed within a company site or to any other site anywhere in the world, by using networks or just duplicating the expert system on standalone hardware.
- *Training.* The explanation capabilities of expert systems are such that they often function as training systems: users can see the chain of reasoning underlying their decisions and hence gain a better understanding of the problem domain.
- *Competitive edge.* Expert systems will often give a company a competitive edge, owing to highly increased response speeds, accuracy of decisions, and so on.
- *Cost reduction.* The cost of providing expertise per user is lower; computers do not get paid large salaries for sharing their knowledge, or consume significant resources apart from energy and maintenance costs.

### *Advantages to the user*

- *Knowledge accessibility.* The expertise is always available on any computer hardware.
- *Training.* The value of training can be an advantage to both employer and employee.

- *Consistency*. The user will know that advice given is not subject to human fallibility. The expert system is not likely to have off-days, or feel sick, or have too many other things on its mind.

## 1.9 Expert systems as decision support systems

Decision support systems (DSS) are a branch of operational research (OR), which evolved from the need to apply quantitative techniques to the solution of complex management problems. Much of the success of OR in the last three decades has been due to traditional OR approaches, which require numerous, long-winded calculations. DSS are traditionally defined as the application of OR and computing to supporting the management decision process. The main characteristics of DSS are as follows:

- Provide management with rapid access to information that can be used in the decision-making process.
- Integrate OR techniques with information processing software.
- Improve the impact of the management decision process by extending the capability of managers who make those decisions.
- Help management deal with unstructured problems (i.e. problems that cannot be solved by structured OR techniques alone).

### *Differences between DSS and expert systems*

Many people confuse the relationship between DSS and expert systems. DSS support decision makers using data processing and/or OR techniques; expert systems, in contrast, can make the decisions themselves. In practice, however, they would often be used for advisory purposes: that is, with the user retaining control, authority and responsibility, and only consulting the system for advice or confirmation. There are other distinguishing characteristics, as follows:

- Expert system solutions are not applied to problems requiring the mathematical optimisation techniques that are applied to traditional DSS.
- Expert systems can be applied to problems whose objectives and constraints are difficult to specify in quantitative terms.
- Expert systems are effective for eliciting alternatives as part of the solution process; these may include what-if scenarios etc. This is due to the reasoning capabilities of expert systems.

DSS often aid human decision making by some qualitative or quantitative analysis, whereas expert systems try to replace the human expertise or expert. The differences between DSS and expert systems are summarised in Table 1.3.

Table 1.3 *Decision support systems versus expert systems*

| *Attributes* | *DSS* | *Expert systems* |
|---|---|---|
| Objectives | Assist decision making | Copy and replace human capabilities |
| Major orientation | Decision making | Transfer of expertise |
| Decision maker | User and/or system | System |
| Problem domain | Broad, complex | Narrow |
| World view | Open | Closed |
| Query direction | Human queries | System queries human |
| Data manipulation | Numerical/symbolic | Symbolic |
| Mathematical models | Incorporated | – |

## Exercises

1. What do you see as being the primary objective of AI research: the human mind or an intelligent machine? Give reasons to support your answer.
2. Research and discuss the Turing Test for AI. Do you think any of the current AI systems could pass the Turing Test? Give reasons for your answer.
3. Discuss areas where you think expert systems could contribute to the productivity and profitability of an organisation.
4. Management services have in the past depended upon mathematical techniques for dealing with complex managerial problems such as scheduling and planning. Expert system techniques are now sometimes used instead. Why?
5. Describe, in your own words, what you think would make computer software "intelligent."
6. Discuss two potentially negative effects on society of the development of AI techniques.
7. Why did the general problem solver program discussed earlier in this chapter fail?

### *References and further reading*

Bramer, M. A. (1986) *Research and Development in Expert Systems III*, Cambridge: Cambridge University Press.

Lighthill, J. (1972) *The Lighthill Report on AI*, Science Research Council Publication.

DTI (1992) *KBS: Survey of UK Applications*, Touche Ross and Co.

Feigenbaum, E. A. (1982) *Knowledge Engineering in the 1980s*, Dept. of Computer Science, Stanford University, Stanford, CA.

Lenat, D. and Guha, H. (1991) *Building Large Knowledge Based Systems: the CYC Project*, Reading, MA: Addison-Wesley.

McDermott, J. (1982) R1: A rule based configurer of computer systems. *Artificial Intelligence*, vol. 19, no. 1.

Newell, A. and Simon, H. A. (1976) Computer science as empirical inquiry. *Communications of the ACM*, vol. 19, pp. 113–126.

Newell, A., Sham, J. C. and Simon, H. A. (1963) Empirical explorations with the Logic Theory Machine: a case study in heuristics. In *Computers & Thought*, ed. E. A. Feigenbaum, New York: McGraw-Hill.

Rich, E. (1992) *Artificial Intelligence*, 2nd edition, New York: McGraw-Hill.

Shortliffe, E. H (1976) *Computer Based Medical Consultations*, New York: Elsevier.

Turing, A. M. (1950) Computing machinery and intelligence. *Mind*, vol. 59.

Waterman, D. (1986) *A Guide to Expert Systems*, Reading, MA: Addison-Wesley.

Whitehead, A. N. and Russell, B. (1910–13) *Principia Mathematica*, vol. 1, Cambridge: Cambridge University Press.

CHAPTER 2

# Basic concepts of expert systems

**Objectives**

In this chapter you will learn:

- to distinguish between knowledge, information and data;
- to distinguish between algorithms and heuristics;
- to understand the characteristics of expert systems and their relationship to AI;
- to understand the state space search paradigm;
- to gain familiarity with the software tools used for developing an expert system.

## 2.1 Introduction

Personal computers have had a phenomenal impact on the business community over the last decade. Word processors, spreadsheets and databases provided the software tools for manipulating data and information. Other less well known software products also began appearing during the late 1980s, suitable for manipulating knowledge, called *expert systems*. Unlike conventional software, expert systems process knowledge – the former process data. The purpose of expert systems was to emulate human experts at work by attempting to reason with knowledge. Human expertise can be an expensive commodity – the services of doctors or solicitors do not come cheap! Consequently, expert systems have made a significant impact in recent years. This chapter examines the basic concepts of expert systems and identifies the distinguishing characteristics of this technology with conventional software. The following help desk scenario introduces some of the concepts.

### *A help desk scenario for PC faults*

Suppose that a woman bought a new computer from a computer shop only to discover when she arrived home that it was not working properly. She might telephone the vendor for technical assistance. Eventually, she might speak to an expert who would attempt to diagnose the fault by asking a series of questions such as "does the PC power light appear?" or "is the cable properly connected?" etc. These questions provide the expert with data. The answers given would enable the expert to use knowledge about this domain to draw conclusions about what the likely fault is, and from that diagnosis to suggest possible remedies.

An expert system will apply rules to the data in the same way as the human expert. The human expert is using *rules of thumb* or *heuristics* to diagnose the fault. These heuristics may be stored as rules such as "if the PC power light is off, then check that the power switch is on" etc. As a result of familiarity gained by experience, the expert has learned how and when to apply these heuristics. This is the dictionary definition of *knowledge*. Moreover, when an expert applies this knowledge, he or she may deduce new knowledge from the answers to the questions, or data supplied. For example, if the power switch is off then the power light will not illuminate. The new knowledge that "the power light will not illuminate" has been inferred from the data given: that is, "the power switch is off." This process would take place in much the same way when a medical expert is diagnosing a patient illness, or when a finance consultant is advising a client on an appropriate choice of investment.

### *What are expert systems?*

An expert system is a program that attempts to mimic human expertise by applying inference methods to a specific body of knowledge. This body of knowledge is called the *domain*. It is important to be clear about the distinction between data, information and knowledge. Data is nothing more than a group of alphabetic symbols. Thus the following is a list of data items:

a. 6
b. 6.0
c. –6
d. Oasis

The item list from a to d is a group of symbols, which mean nothing on their own. It is only when some context is added to these items that they have any benefit: this is called *information*. The items in the list below have now been converted to information:

a. £6
b. 6.0 marks awarded in the competition
c. –6°C
d. Oasis are a successful UK rock group

Each item in this list has been converted from a set of alphabetic characters (data) to an item of meaningful information. Thus, the presence of the £ symbol in front of item a refers to a sum of money. Item b represents marks given in some competition. Item c refers to a (very cold) temperature, and the final item refers to a successful UK rock group named Oasis.

Now consider the following list of items. These are items of knowledge in that they are gained from experience. Notice that each item expresses relationships between premises and rules for manipulating them.

a. It is raining, therefore I shall get wet!
b. The temperature is –60°C, so it is cold!
c. The engine of the car is hot; it must have been recently used!
d. Oasis are affluent musicians.

Knowledge differs from information because information is passive in the sense that it does not give rise to further generations of information. Knowledge, conversely, is active in that it can give rise to further generations of information. For example, in item a of the list above, experience tells us that if we go out in the rain then we will get wet. That is, we derive the information that we will get wet from the known information that it is raining. This knowledge is frequently represented in the form of rules, although as will be seen later there are other ways of representing knowledge. Similarly, item d stating that Oasis are affluent musicians has been inferred from the experience of knowing that successful rock groups usually become millionaires.

---

### Self-assessment exercise

Consider the following statement: "Bananas are usually yellow." Would you describe this statement as knowledge or information?

---

## 2.2 AI

Expert systems owe their origin to the field of AI. One of the pioneers of AI, Marvin Minsky, defined AI as: "The field of study that is attempting to build systems which if attempted by people would be considered intelligent" (Minsky 1975). AI is a broad field containing many application areas, some of which are shown in Fig. 2.1. This book is concerned only with the study of expert systems. Cawsey (1998) examines several of these AI application areas in some detail.

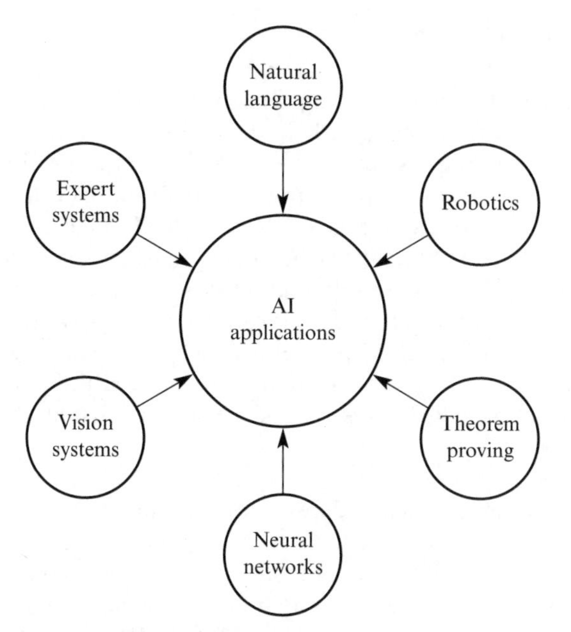


**Figure 2 .1** Some applications of AI

### *Heuristics*

Expert systems are considered as a branch of AI because the method of problem solving is predominantly based on heuristics. This is very different from the conventional program paradigm where *algorithms* are used to solve problems. An algorithm is a step-by-step procedure that solves a category of problems. For example, the processing of a company payroll uses algorithms, perhaps using a step-by-step procedure on the input data such as employee hours worked, overtime rate, etc., to generate output as payslips for employees. The steps in this procedure involve direct manipulation of numeric data to produce information. Most conventional applications use algorithmic methods for problem solving.

Heuristics, on the other hand, solve a problem by trial and error guided by some reference to a predetermined goal. The computer fault diagnostic help desk discussed earlier in this chapter is a case in point, but there are many other examples that may be encountered. For example, a motorist searching a multi-storey car park for a parking space would not use an algorithm to find a space. After all, there is no guarantee that whatever procedure is adopted a parking space will be found. The motorist may, for instance, drive to the top level first rather than search each level in turn, but there is no guarantee that this approach will work.

## 2.3 State space search

Solutions to these problems are exemplified by a search through possible states. In the case of the computer fault help desk, the search involves finding the cause of the fault; in the case of the car park the problem is finding an empty space. The solution to this type of problem is found from knowing how to move from an initial state to a final, or goal, state. To take another example, a chess game involves an initial state (the initial board configuration) and a final state (checkmate). Success requires knowledge of the correct sequence of moves to arrive at the final state. This is called a *state space search* and it characterises the nature of most AI problems. Since this involves a search among alternative choices, it is possible to represent the resulting search space as a hierarchical structure called a *tree*. The next example illustrates this point.

**Example**

Suppose a travelling sales representative wanted to find a route from initial state A to goal state F, from among the network of roads shown in Fig. 2.2. These states could represent cities in the UK. For example, the initial state (A) might represent the city Sheffield and the goal state might represent the city Cardiff (F). The intermediate states such as B, C and so on may be cities passing through a possible route, such as Manchester, Birmingham, and so on. For simplicity, all cities have been denoted by capital letters A, B, C, etc.

From the diagram of the road network, in Fig. 2.2, a tree diagram can be produced as shown in Fig. 2.3. A tree is a hierarchical structure that consists of nodes and branches which connect the nodes in the tree. Hence, each node in the tree diagram depicts a city, and each branch is depicted by a road. The solution path runs from the initial state shown, along the branches of the tree, and terminates at the nodes marked "goal state". Note that it is possible to have more that one solution to an AI problem, since there is more than one way to get from the initial state to the goal state.

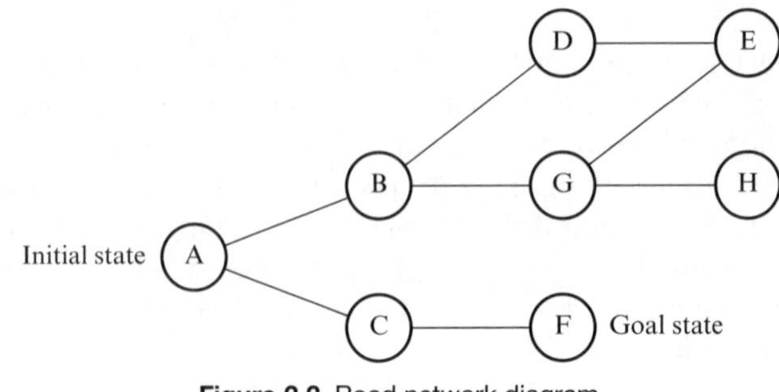


**Figure 2.2** Road network diagram

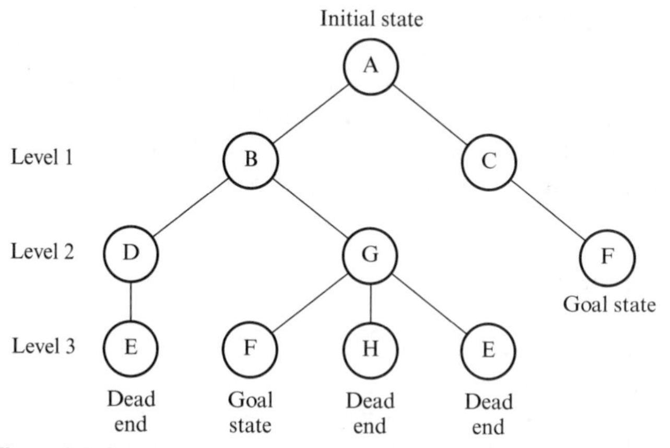


**Figure 2.3** Search tree for travelling sales representative road network

## *Search techniques*

It is not difficult to see how rapidly the search space will grow as the number of nodes increases. This has always been a major stumbling block to large AI problems such as playing chess. This phenomenon is called the *combinatorics explosion*. To deal with the combinatorics explosion, a number of heuristic techniques have been developed. Techniques for searching fall into two categories: *blind search* and *heuristic search*.

### *Blind search*

With the blind search technique an ordering scheme is chosen and applied until a solution is found or, if not, until the search space is exhausted. There are two such procedures for conducting a blind search: depth first and breadth first. With a *depth-first* procedure, the search begins at the root node and continues to search each node at the next lower level, thus moving deeper and deeper down the tree until a solution is found, or the search space is exhausted. When a dead-end node is found the search mechanism backtracks. Thus, for a depth-first search applied to the transport problem in Fig. 2.3, the following happens. Starting from node A, the next lower level is node B: no solution is found so the next lower level inspected is D; again no solution is found and so the next lower level is a terminal node or dead end. Since no solution is found, the search procedure continues by backtracking to node B. Again the search process continues by descending down to the next level at node G; no solution is found so node F is inspected next, which is the required goal. The procedure now terminates since a solution is found.

The *breadth-first* procedure is such that the nodes of the search tree are generated and examined level by level rather than depth by depth. Thus a search on the tree shown in Fig. 2.3 would result in the following trace. Node A would be followed by node B being inspected. B is not a goal node, so the next node on this level is searched. The next node to be generated is C; this is not a goal state node, and since there are no more nodes at this level, the next level is now searched beginning with D. This is not a goal state node so the next node G is generated on this level. Again this is not a goal node; node F is then generated, which is the goal state. The breadth-first procedure then terminates as expected.

---

### Self-assessment exercise

Count the number of nodes that are inspected by the depth-first and breadth-first procedures for the problem depicted in Fig. 2.2. Which method is better for this problem? Can you suggest what tree structure is likely to be better for applying the breadth-first rather than depth-first procedure?

---

#### *Heuristic search*

A blind search does not make any use of the knowledge about the problem to guide the search. In complex problems, such searches will often require enormous resources to counter the combinatorics explosion. Heuristic searches use domain-specific knowledge to traverse the search space. This contrasts with blind search techniques that use "brute force" methods to scan the alternative nodes without any regard to domain knowledge. For example, a chess game heuristic might be to move in such a way as to maximise the number of pieces taken from your opponent. This sounds as though it may be a good "rule of thumb"; however, it may not always succeed. The goal state in a chess game is not to have more pieces than your opponent, although having more pieces will often strengthen the chances of winning. In the travelling sales representative problem, one straightforward method for choosing paths is to apply an "evaluation function." The evaluation function generates each node and then pursues the path that has the least expected cost. This might be the total cost of travelling from one node to the next. Typically, the evaluation function calculates the cost from the root to the particular node that is being examined, and, using heuristics, estimates the cost from that node to the goal. This will serve as a guide as to whether to proceed along that path or to try another among those examined thus far.

## 2.4 Using rules to represent knowledge

Expert systems differ from conventional programs by processing knowledge rather than information. This knowledge is frequently represented in a computer in the form of *rules*; they store the heuristics that guide the human expert. For example, a typical rule used by a house mortgage expert might be:

IF the applicant likes the house
AND the house is worth a survey
THEN advise the applicant to apply for a loan.

Rules would usually be expressed in the form:

IF condition(s)
THEN actions(s)

The action(s) are executed when the condition(s) of the rule are satisfied. The rules created in this way are collectively called the *knowledge base*. The majority of expert systems are developed using rules, and for this reason are called *rule-based* systems. However, not all expert systems are amenable to rules; other representation schemes such as *frames*, *semantic networks* or *logic* may be used as alternatives. Knowledge representation schemes are discussed in Chapter 3.

## 2.5 Inference

The real forte of an expert system is its capacity to make inferences. This is precisely what makes an expert system *intelligent*. Inference is the drawing of conclusions from premises. Hence, for an inference to occur there must be both a premise and a conclusion that is drawn from that premise. There are various forms of inference, deductive and inductive inference being two of the most commonly used. For an example of deductive inference, consider the following propositions:

Rachel is a programmer; (1)
All programmers are happy, (2)
therefore Rachel is happy. (3)

### *Deductive inference*

Propositions (1), (2) and (3) form an example of *deductive* inference. The conclusion (3) in this example is a logical consequence of, or can be deduced from, the premises (1) and (2). In this example, the conclusion can be inferred solely from the information given. This deduction is a consequence of *entailment* that leads to a form of reasoning that is mathematically exact. This means that if the premises are true, then the conclusion is guaranteed also to be true.

### *Inductive inference*

Now consider the following propositions:

| | |
|---|---|
| All animals eat; | (4) |
| therefore all kangaroos eat. | (5) |

On first inspection, it might be tempting to assume that the above conclusion (5), namely "all kangaroos eat", follows by deduction from the premise (4). However, this assumption is false for the premise given says nothing about whether or not a kangaroo is an animal. Human beings would draw upon their own real-world knowledge about animals to assume the truth of this premise (that a kangaroo is an animal). Hence, the conclusion (5) does not have the same mathematical exactness that the previous conclusion (3) had. For the conclusion (5) to be true we would have to *induce* the assumption that "an animal is a kangaroo" to the given premise (4) from common-sense knowledge of the world. For this reason, such inferences are called *inductive* inferences. This form of inference lacks the mathematical exactness of deduction. However, inductive inference is common in expert systems because it does match human inference in the real world.

---

## Self-assessment exercise

What would you add to premise (4) to convert it into a deductive inference?

---

### *Declarative and procedural knowledge*

The problem-solving approach of AI and expert systems is predominantly *declarative*. This means that such problems are characterised by *declaring* what needs to be done in order to find a solution. As an example, consider the propositions given below:

| | |
|---|---|
| Dave likes tennis. | (6) |
| Everything that Dave likes, Janice likes. | (7) |

Clearly, deductive reasoning leads to the conclusion that Janice likes tennis given the above premises. The rule (7) and fact (6) that are given lead to this conclusion. This is the declarative paradigm. Note that the conclusion is found by reasoning with what is given, not by explicitly programming the computer on how to reach the solution. An example of a language that uses the declarative paradigm is the AI language PROLOG. The word PROLOG is taken from the words PROgramming LOGic; it contains an in-built logic to deduce solutions to problems of the declarative type.

This contrasts with the conventional algorithmic paradigm that describes how a *procedure* is executed by explicitly describing the steps involved to reach a solution. Thus the conventional program paradigm is *procedural* as opposed to the AI paradigm, which is predominantly declarative.

### The inference engine

Even when it is possible to represent domain knowledge as rules, a human expert would have to know not only which rules to apply, but also in what order they should be applied to solve a particular problem. Similarly, an expert system would need to decide which rules, and in what order, should be selected for evaluation. To do this, an expert system uses an *inference engine*. The inference engine is a program that interprets the rules in the knowledge base in order to draw conclusions. Two main alternative strategies are used with rule-based systems: *backward chaining* and *forward chaining*. A particular inference engine may adopt either or both.

A backward-chaining inference engine is "goal orientated" in the sense that it tries to prove a goal or rule conclusion by confirming the truth of all of its premises. As an example, consider the following typical rule taken from the MYCIN expert system:

IF the stain of the organism is gram negative
AND the morphology of the organism is rod
AND the aerobicity of the organism is anaerobic
THEN there is strongly suggestive evidence (0.8) that the class of the organism is Enterobacteriaceae.

To prove this rule using backward chaining, the inference engine tries to prove the conclusion of the rule by attempting to prove each premise leading to the rule conclusion. These premises may themselves be conclusions of other rules, in which case MYCIN would then apply the same process to such premises, or the values of these premises may be data supplied by the user from clinical observations. In this way, a chain of inference steps will lead to a value for the goal being found. In contrast, a forward-chaining inference engine starts from the other end. It examines the current state of the knowledge base and finds those rules whose premises can be satisfied from known given data, and then adds the conclusions of those rules to the knowledge base. It then re-examines the complete knowledge base and repeats the process, which can now progress further since new information has been added. Both the backward and forward inference processes will consist of a chain of steps that can be traced by the expert system. This enables expert systems to explain their reasoning. Chapter 5 examines inference in more detail.

### Explanation facilities

The ability to explain their reasoning processes is a key feature of expert systems. However, for many expert systems, the ability to explain may amount to nothing more than a trace of conclusions obtained during a consultation with the system. This means that the explanation facility would enable a user to find out how the system arrived at its conclusions, or perhaps why the system is asking for an answer to a particular question. Such explanation facilities provide the user with a means of understanding the system's behaviour. This is important because a consultation with a human expert will often require some explanation. Many people would not always accept the answers of an expert without some form of justification. Moreover, there is a greater need for explanation than in a conventional system using algorithmic methods because of the uncertainty underlying human expertise. For example, a medical expert providing a diagnosis of a patient would be expected to explain the reasoning behind his or her conclusions: the uncertain nature of his decision may demand a detailed explanation so that the patient concerned is aware of any risks, alternative treatments, etc. The same applies in the case of management decisions: a means of explicitly describing risks or an explanation of the steps leading to a decision or alternative. "What-if" scenarios are a useful decision support tool for management. Chapter 8 looks at explanation facilities in more detail.

## 2.6 Tools for building expert systems

Special-purpose languages such as Lisp and PROLOG are used for developing general AI applications. However, building expert systems from scratch with these languages requires a detailed knowledge of the language, and is labour intensive. For this reason programs called *expert system shells* are mostly used for building expert systems. Shells have long offered an easy starting point for expert system building because they are expert systems that have been emptied of their rules. This means that developers can concentrate on building only the knowledge base without having to worry about other things such as the inference engine. Although they can be very useful, shells suffer from a lack of flexibility in that it is difficult to modify or change the way they work with regard to both representation of knowledge and the inference mechanism. AM for Windows 95,[1] previously known as Crystal, and Level 5 Object[2] are two of the most commonly used shells in the UK. Other tools for building expert systems are called *AI environments*, or *toolkits*. These are hybrid tools used by experienced developers. The pie chart shown in Fig. 2.4

---

[1] AM for Windows 95 © Intelligent Environments Ltd, Sunbury on Thames, Middlesex.
[2] Level 5 Object © Information Builders Inc., Wembley, Middlesex.

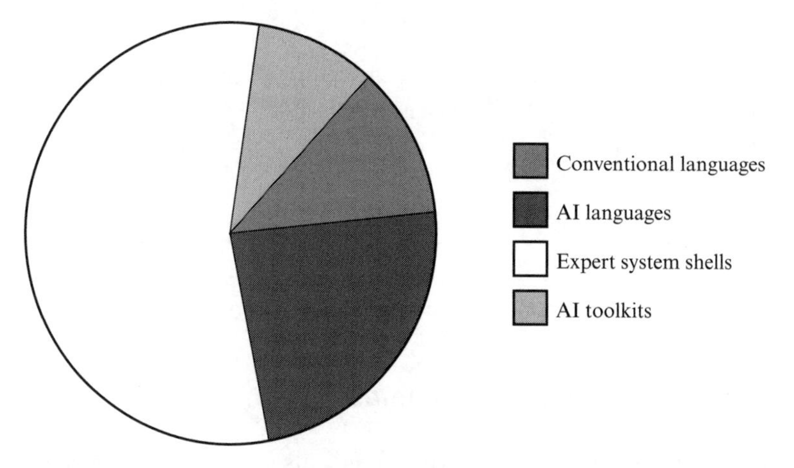


**Figure 2.4** Pie chart for expert system tools percentages in the UK (Edwards 1990)

indicates the distribution of expert system software tools as used in the UK (Edwards 1990) for expert system development. As the pie chart shows, shells are frequently used in the UK. This is because many expert systems developed in the UK are small systems, typically requiring development times of less than 3 months. However, in the USA expert systems tend to be larger integrated applications predominantly developed using toolkits, requiring development times of 12 months or more.

## 2.7 The user interface

An expert system user interface is normally of a highly interactive nature, to reflect the form of dialogue that takes place between a client and a human expert. The expert system user interface will not only enable the user to answer questions but also allow the user to interrupt its running operation by asking for explanations. So, whenever the system is asking the user a question, the user could interrupt the system by asking for an explanation of why the system is asking that question. For example, a user of a medical expert system might want to know why the system asks for the "patient's age." This type of interrogative is called a "Why" explanation. Another type of explanation interrogative is the "How" question. This is normally used to question how the system arrived at a particular decision. For example, if a user of a medical expert system is told that the patient has meningitis, the user might want to know how the system arrived at this conclusion. Designing interfaces for expert systems is further examined in Chapter 8.

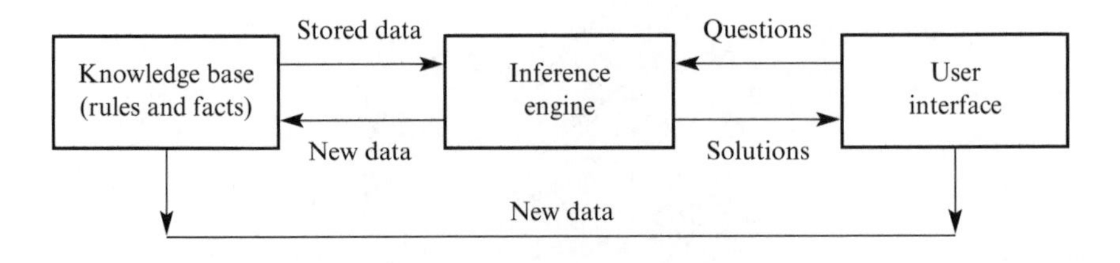


**Figure 2.5** Basic architecture of an expert system

## 2.8 Architecture of expert systems

The relationships between the various concepts discussed in this chapter are illustrated in Fig. 2.5. This diagram shows the basic architecture of an expert system.

### *Learning capabilities*

Another feature that distinguishes expert systems from conventional systems is their capability to learn. Some can even learn without user assistance, through a process called *rule induction* (see Chapter 6), which analyses statistical data about a problem domain in order to form new rules. Such techniques can be applied most effectively to well-defined problem domains. Many expert system building tools provide "induction engine" software that is capable of generating rules from the examples given. These issues are discussed in more detail in Chapter 6.

## 2.9 Summary comparison of expert systems with conventional programs

The characteristics that distinguish expert systems from conventional systems are summarised in Table 2.1.

Table 2.1 *Comparison of expert systems and conventional programs*

| *Characteristic* | *Expert system* | *Conventional system* |
|---|---|---|
| Underlying paradigm | Heuristic. Usually implemented using state space search. Solution steps implicit (i.e. not determined by programmer). Solution, if found, not always guaranteed optimal or correct. Usually declarative problem-solving paradigm | Algorithmic. Solution steps explicitly written by programmer. Correct answers given. Procedural problem-solving paradigm |
| Method of operation | Reasons with symbols. For example, infers conclusions from known premises in order to diagnose a patient illness. Inference engine is used to decide the order in which premises are evaluated | Predominantly manipulates data. For example, sorting, calculating and storing data processed to produce information such as payslips for a company payroll system |
| Processing unit | Knowledge. This may be represented in the form of rules. Knowledge is active in that an expert system can reason with knowledge to infer new knowledge from given data | Data. Typically represented in the form of arrays or records in languages like C or COBOL. Data is passive in that it does not give rise to further generations of data |
| Control mechanism | Inference engine is usually separate from domain knowledge | Data or information and control usually integrated together |
| Fundamental components | Inference + knowledge | Algorithm + data |
| User interface | Highly interactive. Usually takes form of question and answer session | Variable |
| Explanation capability | Yes. An explicit trace of the chain of steps underlying the reasoning processes. Would typically enable a user to find out how the system arrived at its conclusions or perhaps why the system is asking for an answer to a particular question | No |
| Learning capability | Yes, but limited | No |

## Exercises

1. Explain what is meant by the term *heuristic*. Give some examples of heuristics from two different application domains.
2. Expert systems can make mistakes. True or false?
3. Why are expert systems considered to be a branch of AI?
4. Expert systems are capable of explaining their reasoning processes. Describe the difference between a "How" and a "Why" explanation using an example domain to illustrate your answer.
5. Describe five application domains where you think expert systems might be helpful.
6. Discuss whether or not the following propositions are inferences:
   (a) Rhiannon inferred that the cat was hungry.
   (b) If it rains then I will get wet.
   (c) Nobody wins; therefore nobody should play.
   (d) The stage light dimmed; then the curtain fell.
   (e) I think therefore I am.
7. Examine the following inferences and discuss their correctness with regard to logic:
   (a) Cardiff is in Wales; therefore Cardiff is in the United Kingdom.
   (b) Tweety is a bird; no birds can sing; therefore Tweety cannot sing.

## *References and further reading*


Cawsey, A. (1998) *The Essence of Artificial Intelligence*, Hemel Hempstead: Prentice Hall.

Darlington, K. (1996) Basic expert systems. *British Computer Society ITIN*, vol. 8.4.

Doukidis, G. and Whittley, E. A. (1989) *Developing Expert Systems*, Bromley: Chartwell-Bratt.

Durkin, J. (1994) *Expert Systems: Design and Development*, London: Macmillan.

Dutta, S. (1995) *Knowledge Processing and Applied AI*, Oxford: Butterworth–Heinemann.

Edwards, J. S. (1990) *Building Knowledge Based Systems*, London: Pitman Press.

Giarratano, J. C. and Riley, G. D. (1994) *Expert Systems: Principles & Programming*, 2nd edition, Boston: PWS Kent.

Jackson, P. (1992) *Introduction to Expert Systems*, Reading, MA: Addison-Wesley.

Minsky, M. (1975) A framework for representing knowledge. In *The Psychology of Human Vision*, ed. Patrick Winston, New York: McGraw-Hill, pp. 211–217.

Rich, E. (1992) *Artificial Intelligence*, 2nd edition, New York: McGraw-Hill.

CHAPTER 3

# Knowledge representation

**Objectives**

In this chapter you will learn:

- to be aware of desirable features for representing knowledge;
- to understand how knowledge is represented as production rules;
- to understand how knowledge is represented in structured object format;
- to understand how knowledge is represented in logic format;
- to compare and contrast the main methods of representing knowledge;
- to identify appropriate representation schemes(s) for building expert systems.

## 3.1 Introduction

The pioneers of AI discovered that intelligent behaviour is not so much due to the methods of reasoning, as it is dependent on the knowledge available to reason with. According to R. J. Brachman (1988):

> A widely recognised goal of AI is the creation of artefacts (usually software programs) that can emulate humans in their ability to reason symbolically, as exemplified in typical AI domains such as planning, natural language understanding, diagnostics and tutoring. Currently, most of this work is predicated on the belief that intelligent systems can be constructed from explicit, declarative knowledge bases, which in turn are operated on by general formal reasoning mechanisms. This fundamental hypothesis of AI means that knowledge representation and reasoning – the study of formal ways of extracting information from symbolically represented knowledge – is of central importance to the field.

Knowledge can be represented in a variety of ways. These methods of representing knowledge are described in later sections. It is important to look first at some desirable features of any knowledge representation scheme. Some of these features are:

- To ensure completeness. In other words, the representation should support the acquisition of all aspects of the knowledge.
- To ensure representations are concise. This should allow efficient acquisition so that knowledge is stored compactly and is easily retrieved.
- To ensure computational efficiency. It should be possible to use the knowledge rapidly and without the need for excessive computation.
- To ensure transparency. The representation should be such that it is possible to understand its behaviour and how it arrives at conclusions.
- To make the important things explicit, and suppress detail but keep it available in case it is required in future.

There is no single representation scheme that embodies all the above characteristics. Each of the representation schemes that will be discussed in this chapter has turned out to be suitable for certain types of application domain. Rule-based systems were briefly described in Chapter 2; they are now examined in a little more detail.

## 3.2 Production rules

The majority of expert systems use rules, sometimes called *productions*, to represent knowledge. The popularity of rules is due to the easy way in which they are used. The rules are usually expressed in the general form:

*if* condition(s)
*then* action(s)

The *if* portion, or left-hand side, describes a problem-solving situation, in the form of a set of conditions, sometimes called *antecedents*. These antecedents must be true in order for this rule to be applicable. The *then* portion, or right-hand side, describes the set of actions, sometimes called *consequents*, that follow if the rule is applicable.

### Example

*if* speed of car is too fast
*then* take your foot off the accelerator.

The above example shows that *if* the specific condition "speed of car is too fast" is met, *then* the action part is invoked. Rules may involve several conditions and/or several actions, which can be combined with the use of AND, called *conjunction*, and OR, called *disjunction*. The following example shows two conditions that make use of conjunction.

**Example**

*if* room is cool
  *and* light is poor
    *then* best choice of house plant is ivy;

## Self-assessment exercise

Write down the premises and conclusion in the following statement:

*if* the weather is wet *and* I have an umbrella *then* I will travel to work by bus.

### *Advantages of rules*

The following factors have contributed to the widespread use of rules in expert systems. They are:

- *Simplicity*. Rules form a good psychological model for knowledge representation because they closely relate to human reasoning. This makes rule-based systems easy to build in comparison with other methods for representing knowledge.
- *Modularity*. This means that blocks of rules can be independently written and added to a rule base, and checked for correctness. So rule-based expert systems can be broken down into easily manageable components for development. It is this feature that enables knowledge bases to be constructed incrementally, step by step.
- *Explanation*. Rule-based systems provide simple transparent explanation facilities. These facilities will be discussed in more detail in Chapter 8.
- *Handling uncertainty*. A number of techniques have been developed that allow knowledge about uncertainty to be contained within rules. This theme will be explored in some detail in Chapter 7.

Rules can also be used to express different types of knowledge. For example, heuristic knowledge, domain knowledge and procedural knowledge can all be represented using rules. Examples of each follow.

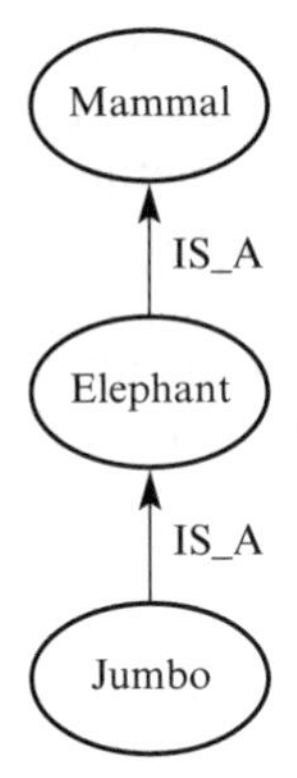


**Figure 3.2** Example of inheritance using semantic networks

### *Advantages of inheritance*

There are several advantages of inheritance, as follows:

- It uses less memory because many relationships need not be explicitly stated.
- Inheritance enables the grouping of similar objects.
- Networks are easier to update since one node can inherit relations from ascendant nodes.

---

## Self-assessment exercise

Draw links and nodes in a semantic network to describe how a dog called Rover and another dog called Ben have four legs.

---

Semantic networks are not very useful in practice because they are restricted to representing declarative knowledge and cannot represent procedural knowledge, and whilst it is possible to create any object or concept, there are no standards for forming semantic networks. This means that their form can vary from system to system. Frames are an alternative object-based representation, which have now almost completely replaced the use of semantic networks in practical systems.

## 3.4 Frames

Marvin Minsky first conceived the concept of *frame* in 1975 when he defined a frame as follows:

> A frame is a structured piece of information about properties, characteristics or features of an object, act or event.

```
FRAME animal;
        NAME                    FILLER VALUE
        IS_A                    sentient_being
        NUMBER_OF_LEGS          default = 4
        IS_FURRY                default = true
```

**Figure 3.3** Animal frame template

A frame serves as a kind of template for holding related clusters of data. This data is usually stored in slots. The slots are simply attributes of that object. For example, the frame for an object called an animal might have the slots shown in Fig. 3.3.

The slot values in a frame can be of three different kinds:

1. Named slots in a frame may have filler values that are data items, for example the NUMBER_OF_LEGS slot. A data slot is used to store items of data, the type of which may be strings, integers, Boolean values, and so on. A slot may also have a default value assigned to it. This is simply a value given to a slot if no value is found for that slot. In the example of animal the default number value would be 4. This is because the expected value for this slot is generally assumed to be 4. In the named slot called IS_FURRY, the default value is assigned to be true. In other words, an animal is assumed to be furry in the event that nothing else is known about the animal. This is a reasonable assumption since most animals have fur and four legs.
2. Slots in a frame may also be relations, such as the IS_A slot value in the animal frame above. The IS_A slot value is to link object relationships in a hierarchy. This particular slot is defining a relation between the animal frame and a frame called sentient_being. In this way, a hierarchy of animal objects can be defined using frames. See Fig. 3.4.
3. Slots in a frame may also be procedural. For example, consider the dog frame template as shown in Fig. 3.5. A slot has been included in this frame for the amount of daily food intake, called DAILY_FOOD_INTAKE. The possible values taken by this slot could be high, medium or low depending on the weight and height of the dog that is being considered. Large dogs would generally require more food than small dogs. Hence, this slot value could be found from some calculation involving the height and weight of the dog. This slot is said to be procedural in that its value is obtained from some procedural action.

Notice that the first slot in the dog frame says that a dog is an animal. This means that the dog object inherits all the slot values from the animal frame. This is another example of inheritance. As can be seen from the animal frame,

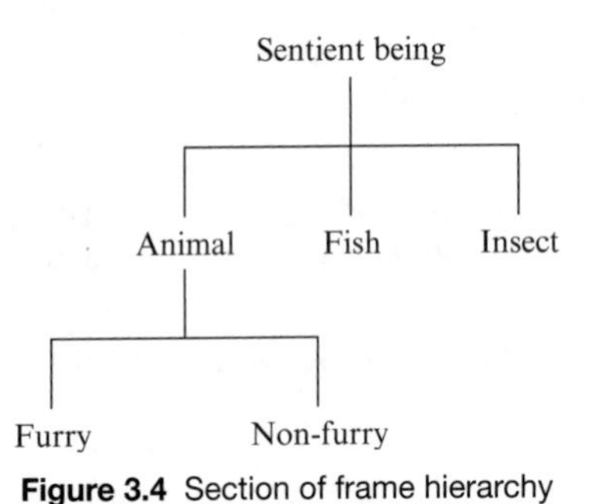


**Figure 3.4** Section of frame hierarchy

the dog will inherit the property that it has four legs. This is because the slot value for NUMBER_OF_LEGS has a default value of 4, in the animal frame. The default value is assumed to be true unless it is overwritten with a different value. Similarly, the slot value for IS_FURRY has a value of true. This means that a dog will be assumed to be a furry animal.

### *Instances of frame objects*

Now consider a particular dog called Rover. The dog frame template in Fig. 3.5 can be used to store particular slot values about Rover as shown in Fig. 3.6.

Since Rover is a dog, then it will inherit all slot values and default values (if any exist). For example, Rover is assumed to be capable of barking, since the general dog frame has a slot for CAN_BARK and a default value of true for this slot. Hence, any descendant slot will inherit this value unless overwritten with a different value. Similarly, Rover also inherits the four-legged slot value from the general animal frame. Notice also that since the height and weight values have been added to this frame, the procedural slot value for DAILY_FOOD_INTAKE has been assigned to high.

FRAME dog;

| SLOT | FILLER VALUE |
|---|---|
| IS_A | animal |
| NAME | – |
| WEIGHT | – |
| HEIGHT | – |
| CAN_BARK | default = true |
| DAILY_FOOD_INTAKE | calculated from height and weight slots when added |

**Figure 3.5** Dog frame template

| Instance of frame Rover | |
| --- | --- |
| SLOT | FILLER VALUE |
| IS_A | dog |
| NAME | Rover |
| WEIGHT | 2.20 |
| HEIGHT | 1.05 |
| CAN_BARK | true (inherited from default dog frame) |
| DAILY_FOOD_INTAKE | high: calculated from knowing the height and weight values |

**Figure 3.6** Frame for the dog named Rover

The hierarchical relationship between the dog called Rover, the dog frame, the animal frame and the sentient being frame is shown in Fig. 3.7.

## 3.5 Logic

Historically, logic has been extensively used in AI programs. The main purpose of logic concerns the soundness or unsoundness of arguments. Typically, an argument consists of statements called *propositions*, from which other statement(s) called *conclusion(s)* are claimed to follow. This is the basis of propositional logic, which is considered in the next section.

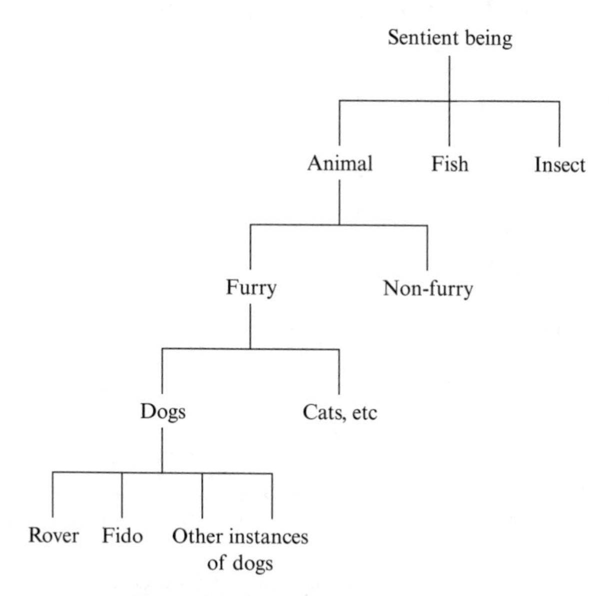


**Figure 3.7** Complete frame hierarchy

### *Propositional logic*

In order to formalise the language of logic, it is necessary to define what is meant by a proposition. A proposition is a sentence that is either true or false. For example, the following are propositions:

"Keith is a happy man" (1)
"All cats are good pets" (2)

Both of the above sentences (1) and (2) are propositions, because each is either true or false. The following phrases are not propositions:

"Amy's pet" (3)
"Oh dear me!" (4)

---

## Self-assessment exercise

According to our definition, which of the following are propositions?

a. Miss Piggy is President.
b. How old are you?
c. $4 - 3 = 6$.

---

Statements in propositional logic are usually expressed symbolically. For example, the following inference:

"If Keith is a happy man then Keith is a teacher"

could be symbolically expressed as:

A Keith is a happy man
B Keith is a teacher

This could be expressed in propositional logic as:

*if* A *then* B

This is written in logic notation as $A \rightarrow B$ (meaning proposition A implies proposition B). This is an example of a rule of inference called *modus ponens*. Put simply, it says that if proposition A is true, and the rule of inference $A \rightarrow B$ is true, then B will also be true.

Propositions can be combined using logical connectives: for example, as in the statement

"If I listen to Bach and the room is warm then I fall asleep"

Rewriting this symbolically:

| | |
|---|---|
| Let A be the proposition | I listen to Bach |
| Let B be the proposition | The room is warm |
| Let C be the proposition | I fall asleep |

Then this can be written in logic notation as:

$$A \wedge B \rightarrow C$$

### *Connective symbols*

The symbols shown in Table 3.1 are used to denote some of the most common connectives used in propositional logic.

Table 3.1 *Connectives used in propositional logic*

| *Symbol* | *Meaning* | *Interpretation* |
|---|---|---|
| ~A | Not A | Negation. Negation of proposition A is true if A is false and vice versa |
| $A \wedge B$ | A and B | Conjunction. A and B only true if A and B are both true, otherwise false |
| $A \vee B$ | A or B | Disjunction. A or B is true if A is true or B is true. |
| $A \rightarrow B$ | A implies B | Implication. If A is true and A implies B is true, then B is true. If A is false and A implies B is true then anything goes. That is, B could be true or false, since implication says nothing about case when A is false |

### *Truth table*

The meanings of the connectives and their results are summarised in Table 3.1. However, a truth table can be used to list all possible truth values. The truth table shown in Table 3.2 includes columns for the connectives described in Table 3.1. Note that digit 1 denotes truth, 0 denotes false.

Table 3.2 *Connectives used in propositional logic truth table*

| *A* | *B* | *~A* | $A \wedge B$ | $A \vee B$ | $A \rightarrow B$ |
|---|---|---|---|---|---|
| 1 | 1 | 0 | 1 | 1 | 1 |
| 1 | 0 | 0 | 0 | 1 | 0 |
| 0 | 1 | 1 | 0 | 1 | 1 |
| 0 | 0 | 1 | 0 | 0 | 1 |

### *Predicate logic*

Propositional logic is inadequate for solving some problems because a proposition has to be treated as a single entity that is either true or false. Predicate logic overcomes this by allowing a proposition to be broken down into two components. These are known as *arguments* and *predicates*. It also allows the use of variables, in addition to supporting the rules of inference derived from propositional logic (i.e. *modus ponens* etc.).

For example, consider the proposition:

Amy has brown hair

This could be written in predicate logic notation as:

HAS(Amy, brown hair)

In the above example, HAS is called the predicate, and the arguments are "Amy" and "brown hair."

Now consider the proposition:

Minsky is a cat

The above can be written in predicate logic as:

IS_A(Minsky, cat)

### *Quantifiers in predicate logic*

Predicate logic also allows for the use of quantifiers. This means that the language can be extended to propositions that refer to a range of a variable. For example, consider the proposition:

*Every man loves a woman*

This can be expressed in predicate logic using quantifiers as:

$$\forall\, x, \text{Man}(x) \rightarrow \exists\, y, \text{ s.t. Woman}(y) \wedge \text{Loves}(x, y)$$

which reads: *for any object x in the world if x is a Man, then there exists an object y, such that y is a woman and x Loves y.*

The quantifier $\forall$ is called the *universal quantifier* since it refers to all objects in the (male) population. The quantifier $\exists$ is called the *existential quantifier* since it refers to at least one object in the (female) population.

Now consider the proposition: every Welshman is a Man. This would be expressed in formal logic as:

$$\forall\, x, \text{Welshman}(x) \rightarrow \text{Man}(x)$$

which reads: *for any object x, if x is a Welshman, then x is a Man*. Then from these two facts we can conclude, using the rules of inference, that the following facts must be true:

$$\forall\, x, \text{Welshman}(x) \rightarrow \exists\, y, \text{s.t. Woman}(y) \wedge \text{Loves}(x, y)$$

That is, every Welshman loves a woman. This example may seem to lead to an obvious conclusion. However, for other examples such intuitive conclusions would be less obvious.

The advantage of formal logic is that there is a set of rules called *rules of inference* by which facts that are known to be true can be used to derive other facts, which must also be true. Furthermore, the truth of any new proposition can be checked, in a well-specified manner, against the facts that are already known to be true. However, it is important to remember that logical inferences will only guarantee the truth of a conclusion if the premises leading to the conclusion are also true.

## 3.6 Hybrid representations

There is no single representation that will be suitable for representing every problem domain. Each representation scheme has advantages and disadvantages. These are summarised in Table 3.3. Sometimes, a hybrid representation scheme may be better than any single scheme. AI programming tools containing rules, frames and logic are now available that can combine representation schemes in a variety of ways. Some of these tools will be studied in more detail in Chapter 6. These tools often work well in practice. For example, within a frame system, the slots may be made to represent predicates and the values and frame names may be considered to be arguments to the predicates, so that logical inference may utilise the knowledge within the frames. This frame system could also contain production rules that use procedural knowledge and heuristics.

## 3.7 Summary

As previously stated, no single representation structure is likely to be satisfactory for all types of application domain. Production rules are ideal for

Table 3.3 *Advantages and disadvantages of representation schemes*

| *Representation scheme* | *Advantages* | *Disadvantages* |
|---|---|---|
| Production rules | Modular, flexible, and well suited to many domains | Difficult to represent descriptive knowledge in a natural way. Also difficult to separate domain knowledge and problem-solving knowledge |
| Logic | Precision. That is, conclusions guaranteed to be correct if premises correct. Allows programs to be declarative – for example, PROLOG | Opaque, poor psychological model. Difficult to represent uncertainty |
| Semantic networks | Object-based representation; therefore permits inheritance | Cannot distinguish between the class of an object and a particular object. Unlike frames no facility to handle procedural knowledge. Presentation and structure for complex systems could become unmanageable |
| Frames | Object-based representation facilitates reusability; frames offer facilities for exception handling and defaults, both of which are not easily handled in logic or other representations | Theoretical difficulties arise from slots in a frame being unrestrained. This means nothing can be certain and so it can be impossible to give universal definitions to objects |

capturing the expert's rules of thumb expertise. Logic is often successful in building fairly small, logically consistent knowledge bases, and frames are well suited to structured object representations. Table 3.4 summarises some of the main characteristics of each of the four schemes discussed in this chapter.

## Exercises

1. Frames are used for capturing knowledge about objects. In what kind of situation would frames not be useful for representing knowledge?
2. Lenat, the CYC project leader, once said that even if two expert systems were written in the same language, or shell, and even if their domains seem to be related, there is no chance of being able usefully to exchange rules between the two systems. Why do you think this is so?

Table 3.4 *Summary of the main characteristics of representation schemes*

| *Representation scheme* | *Basic architecture* | *Method(s) of inference* |
|---|---|---|
| Production rules | Consists of set of rules, database of known facts, and an interpreter. System works by applying known facts to left-hand side of rules; if true, right-hand side fires. Newly discovered fact is added to database. Order in which rules are selected depends on the method of inference | Forward or/and backward chaining. In forward chaining, the interpreter searches the database to see which facts match the left-hand side of the rules. In backward chaining, the interpreter tries to prove a goal by attempting to confirm the conditions leading to the goal |
| Logic | Uses clauses, rules of inference such as *modus ponens* and system output in the form of queries | Resolution |
| Semantic networks | Object-based representation. Uses links and nodes to represent associative knowledge | Inheritance through the links and nodes |
| Frames | Object-based representation. Uses slots for storing attributes. Default values can be assigned to slot values, thus facilitating inheritance. | Inheritance through frame hierarchy. Slot value can be set as default. Uses local slot value to override any parent slot value |

**3.** Convert the following propositions into predicate form:
   (a) Katie likes bananas
   (b) Some chickens can fly
   (c) All men eat pasta
**4.** Convert the following predicates into proposition form:
   (a) IS(Mary, happy)
   (b) IS_A(snake, mammal)
   (c) $\forall x$, Person($x$) $\rightarrow \exists y$, s.t. Woman($y$) $\wedge$ Mother($y$, $x$)
**5.** Construct a semantic network for the following situation: Mari is a Dancer. She was born and lives in London, UK, although her parents are Spanish. She specialises in ballet and Latin American dance. Such combinations are rarely found.
**6.** Write a description of a set of frames describing the situation in question 5. Take care with constructing suitable inherited links.
**7.** List five rules that you might use before you go out to buy a new video recorder. Are these rules heuristics? Justify your answer.

### References and further reading

Beynon-Davis, J. (1991) *Expert Database Systems*, London: McGraw-Hill.

Brachman, R. J. (1988) "I lied about the trees". *AI Magazine*, vol. 6, no.3, 80–93.

Clancey, W. J. (1983) Epistemology of a rule-based expert system: a framework for explanation. *AI Magazine*, vol. 20, no.3, 215–251.

Durkin, J. (1993) *Expert Systems: Design and Development*, London: Macmillan.

Dutta, S. (1995) *Knowledge Processing and Applied AI*, Oxford: Butterworth-Heinemann.

Giarratano, J. C. and Riley, G. D. (1990) *Expert Systems: Principles and Programming*, Boston: PWS Kent.

Lenat, D. and Guha, H. (1991) *Building Large Knowledge Based Systems: the CYC Project,* Reading, MA: Addison-Wesley.

Minsky, M. (1975) A framework for representing knowledge. In *The psychology of human vision*, ed. Patrick Winston, New York: McGraw-Hill, pp. 211–217.

Quillian, M. R. (1968) *Semantic memory*, Cambridge, MA: MIT Press, pp. 227–270.

CHAPTER 4

# Knowledge engineering

**Objectives**

In this chapter you will learn:

- what knowledge engineering is and what a knowledge engineer does;
- to distinguish between knowledge acquisition and knowledge elicitation;
- to recognise the skills required of a knowledge engineer;
- techniques for knowledge elicitation;
- direct interviewing techniques;
- indirect knowledge elicitation techniques.

## 4.1 Introduction

This chapter is concerned with knowledge engineering (KE), a term that was first used by Feigenbaum (1980). In essence, it describes the process of KBS development: knowledge engineering is to KBS as systems analysis is to conventional system development A knowledge engineer is a person who is responsible for knowledge engineering. That person has a responsibility for eliciting knowledge for an expert system. This requires an ability to elicit knowledge from expert(s) by conducting interviews, and/or by other methods, so that the problem domain can be understood. This knowledge then has to be translated into a form that can be recognised for use in a computer.

## 4.2 Skills required for KE

Debenham (1990) identified four essential skills of a knowledge engineer. These are:

1. The ability to recognise knowledge that is accurate and complete. Knowledge has to be verified for correctness, and all possible problem scenarios need to

be investigated thoroughly, giving consideration to all possible outcomes. For example, in a medical diagnostic expert system, the expert may forget to elaborate on a rare case of a particular type of disease because of unfamiliarity. This does not mean that such knowledge can be excluded.

**2.** The ability to represent and process knowledge in a way that is not committed to some particular expert system development tool. The manner in which the knowledge is elicited from the expert and prepared for computer input should be independent of the tool that is used, otherwise there is the danger that the knowledge may be structured to conform to the tool used, rather than model the application domain.

**3.** The ability to design an expert system for maintenance. The knowledge in an expert system is often represented as the expert has pronounced it. This can sometimes have serious consequences for maintenance because, in rule-based systems, the effect of changing one or more rules can have an unpredictable effect on other rules in the knowledge base.

**4.** The ability to design an expert system that can interface naturally with existing conventional systems. Corporate users are highly dependent on large databases or spreadsheet data. Experts often access such data in order to make decisions. Thus, some expert systems proposed for development need to be able to access this data, and/or communicate with other conventional programs, such as databases, spreadsheets, and so on.

## 4.3 Knowledge acquisition and knowledge elicitation

The terms *knowledge elicitation* and *knowledge acquisition* are sometimes used interchangeably. However, there is a distinction between these terms as will now be explained. Knowledge elicitation is the process whereby knowledge about the domain is obtained from the expert. Knowledge acquisition, on the other hand, is the whole process of converting the extracted knowledge into a form suitable for use in an expert system. Guidelines on KE techniques have been published by Hayes-Roth, Waterman and Lenat (1983), who define it as both the discipline that addresses the task of building expert systems, and the tools that support expert system development. They also identify knowledge acquisition to be the major bottleneck in the development of an expert system; the truth of this has been borne out by many expert system developers since the time when they wrote these guidelines. Overall, KE involves knowledge acquisition and four other activities. They are:

**1.** Validation and verification
**2.** Knowledge representation
**3.** Inference
**4.** Explanation and justification

All these activities are discussed in other chapters. This chapter will deal with knowledge acquisition.

## 4.4 Knowledge acquisition

The first task of the knowledge engineer is to gain some familiarity with the application domain by understanding basic terminology and concepts. Such information can often be found in manuals, books, in-house documentation, and so on. However, these sources of knowledge can quickly become dated, and hence interview(s) with a domain expert are often essential. It may also be difficult to get an overview of the domain structure without interviewing an expert, for knowledge obtained in manuals may be dispersed and lack structure. Experts are continuously learning without necessarily updating such knowledge in written documents.

## 4.5 Interviewing

Interviewing is the primary means of acquiring human expertise. Successful interviewing involves planning, preparation, recording and documentation. The same may be true for other forms of interviewing, for example interviewing a job applicant. However, planning and preparation are particularly important for knowledge elicitation interviews, because an expert system is only as good as the quality of the domain knowledge it contains. If the expert has not been adequately briefed, or prepared, then incorrect responses may be given to questions because, perhaps, the context in which the question was asked was incorrect.

Preparation is likely to involve a discussion with the expert about the following factors:

1. A discussion about the purpose and nature of the interview(s). The idea is to set the expert at ease and enable the expert to prepare mentally for the interview.
2. What factors are going to influence progress? For example, the knowledge engineer may state that gaining an understanding of the scope of the domain, or perhaps gaining a knowledge of the expert's tasks, is going to influence progress.
3. Special equipment to be used or arrangements made. For example, should the interview be tape recorded or video recorded, or should an assistant be used to take notes during the interview?
4. Environmental setting of the interview. For example, what type of room should be used, or what time of day should the interview be conducted?

---

## Self-assessment exercise

What are the questions to be asked when an interview is completed?

---

## 4.6 Direct interview techniques

Having prepared the interview(s), the next stage is to conduct the interview(s) successfully. Direct interview techniques fall into three main categories. They are:

- The expert-focused interview (or orientation interview)
- The structured interview
- The thinking aloud interview

### *The orientation interview*

The first interview to be conducted is usually the orientation or focused interview. The purpose of this type of interview is to gain an overview of the application domain. The knowledge engineer (or elicitor) will allow the expert to speak freely about the expertise within the mutually agreed limits of scope and domain view. The elicitor will have already explained what type of information is wanted at this stage (e.g. a global view of the domain under discussion), would only intervene to direct the expert with general questions, and will listen while the expert outlines an area in high-level terms. This technique is used to elicit general (surface area) knowledge about the domain of study.

In using the technique the elicitor may begin by asking general orientation questions such as:

- "Could you describe, in simple terms, what you do?", or
- "What do you consider to be your main task?", or
- "What is your main problem?"

### *The structured interview*

This type of interview is used primarily as a second phase to acquire more depth and fill out levels of detail about the expertise. The knowledge engineer will have already carried out orientation interviews with the expert and hence may use these interviews as an opportunity to clarify and iron out misunderstandings about domain concepts etc. For this reason, the dialogue will be much more of a two-way process in this type of interview, with the expert responding to questions from the knowledge engineer. Ideally, the elicitor allows the expert to follow through the problem while restraining the expert from digressing from the main focus of interest. The expert may be asked questions such as:

- "Why do you get this problem?", or
- "Could you explain how you do this in greater detail?", or
- "I don't understand why you do this?", or
- "What happens here?", and so on.

### *The thinking aloud interview*

Structured interviews sometimes fail to capture all domain knowledge. The thinking aloud interview, as its name suggests, encourages the expert to talk while thinking (Firlej and Hellens 1991). Using this technique, an expert may be given a task similar to one that is commonly met in the expert's problem-solving environment. The expert is asked to verbalise any thoughts on that given task. The thinking aloud interview(s) normally follow the structured interview(s), so that the expert's problem-solving strategies and knowledge gathered from previous interviews can be validated.

## 4.7 Summary of interviewing techniques

The main techniques used for interviewing are summarised in Table 4.1.

## 4.8 Other knowledge elicitation techniques

Direct interview methods may not always lead the expert to divulge the details of how knowledge is used. For example, a decision may depend on many combinations of factors. To verbalise all such possibilities could be difficult and time consuming. Indirect efforts such as machine-based rule induction (Hart 1985) enable the expert to interact directly with an expert system. A number of other knowledge elicitation techniques are now in common use, some of which are briefly described below.

### *Repertory grid*

The psychologist G. Kelly (1955) developed the concept of the repertory grid. It is a representation of the expert's view of a particular problem. It is made up

Table 4.1 *Interview techniques*

| *Interview method* | *Purpose and applicability* | *Some possible problems* | *Some possible remedies* |
|---|---|---|---|
| Orientation | To elicit surface knowledge about a domain. Used in first stage of elicitation | 1. The expert has difficulty recalling information | Try with another view of the domain, one that the expert may find more interesting |
| | | 2. The expert uses too much jargon or perhaps blinds the elicitor with expertise | The expert may be suspicious, or feel uneasy with the elicitor's approach. Ensure adequate preparation and discussion prior to the interview |
| Structured | Used to acquire more depth and detail. The elicitor may probe for detailed explanations of concepts described in an orientation interview. Structured interviews are carried out in the second phase of the interviewing process | 1. Incomplete or missing knowledge<br>2. Inconsistent knowledge | The elicitor will need to probe the expert carefully by asking questions such as: "What happens if the value of a concept is unknown?", or, "Can this condition take any more condition take any more values?", and so on |
| Thinking aloud | Used to confirm assumptions and validate knowledge gathered from previous sessions. Used as a third stage of interviewing | 1. It is difficult to simulate the expert's task in a useful way<br>2. The act of thinking aloud can affect the way the expert works | The expert may feel inhibited. Consider modifying the interview in some way |

of sets of so-called *elements* and constructs. Elements are placed along an axis in a two-dimensional plane. These elements will be familiar objects to the expert, such as a list of persons, or objects such as cars. A construct is a bipolar characteristic that each element under consideration may have. For example, a car will have weight and colour. The typical procedure begins by collecting a set of objects in the domain of the grid. A maximum of 10 is taken. They are then presented in groups of three and the expert is asked to say in what way two of the three are alike, and different from the third. As all the possible combinations of three are presented, the ways in which objects in the fields are distinguished from one another become clear.

### *Observational techniques*

An alternative approach to asking experts what they do is to watch them as they solve problems. A variety of techniques called *protocol analysis* are available.

### *Protocol analysis*

This method is based upon the thinking aloud interview technique. The expert is asked to explain what he or she is doing while carrying out a task. A tape or video recording is collected and later transcribed and analysed. The method has the advantage that the task would be completed exactly as it normally is.

Other techniques for knowledge acquisition include:

- Observation
- Case studies
- Role play

### *Observation*

One of the greatest problems with interviewing is the demand made of the expert's time. This is not the case with observation, because observing the expert at work does not impose any demands additional to the norm. By observing an expert at work, a knowledge engineer can also see realistically how knowledge is used. Observation can also be combined with formal interviewing to enable the knowledge engineer to verify or validate existing domain assumptions.

The disadvantages with observation are that it can be very time consuming and may cover only a limited number of "cases." Also, an expert may feel embarrassed by being observed, and perhaps behave unnaturally. Successful observation techniques therefore require careful analysis of the working environment by making the knowledge engineer as surreptitious as possible.

### *Case studies*

One of the problems with observation is the unpredictability of the types of problems that may arise. This may result in much time being wasted by the knowledge engineer in observing duplicate problems. This can be overcome by using case studies. Here the knowledge engineer can choose cases to be discussed by the expert. As with observation, case studies can be time consuming and expensive because the expert has to consider all cases to cover all eventualities.

### *Role play*

Again this technique can be time consuming and may not cover all possibilities. Role play can also be difficult to administer and requires that a second knowledge engineer be present to be effective.

## 4.9 Difficulties with knowledge acquisition

The problems of knowledge acquisition have often precipitated a bottleneck in the development of expert systems. Table 4.2 lists some of these problems and suggests possible solutions.

---

## Exercises

1. What are the likely problems arising from thinking aloud interviewing? How would you set about overcoming these problems?
2. Search the literature of the last two years to find an example of an expert system used in business. Describe the system briefly and critique it.
3. Explain briefly what a knowledge engineer does and why he or she is necessary.
4. Describe two broad approaches to acquiring knowledge for an expert system.
5. What is protocol analysis? Give an explanation using an example, and give one advantage and one disadvantage of this approach.
6. What do you think is needed for a valuable knowledge elicitation session?
7. A small, private, drift coal-mining company has decided to purchase an expert system shell in order to build a coal-cutting machine fault diagnostics system. The system will be developed with the following objectives in mind. The first is to minimise the downtime of the coal-cutting machines. In addition to this, the system is designed to reduce the technician's load and provide a basis for an active training aid for new technicians. Fast development time is essential. The system will be required to import/export data from spreadsheets in order to find out whether there is excessive overloading on the cutting machines. Finally, diagrams will be required by the system to show the locations of the faults, where to find replacement faulty components, and so on.
   (a) What would be the advantages and disadvantages of using:
      (i) observation
      (ii) case studies
      (iii) role play
      in order to capture the appropriate knowledge for this application domain?

Table 4.2 *The problems of knowledge acquisition*

| *Problem* | *Possible solution* |
|---|---|
| The knowledge engineer has difficulty extracting the rules from the expert – the interactions seem laborious and provide a small payoff | Try to choose an articulate, highly motivated, computer-aware expert. It may be possible to canvass the opinions of the expert's peers for guidance on this. Remember also that the expert needs to be a good communicator |
| The domain expert cannot find enough time for the project | This is a common practical problem; the solution to this is to make sure that the expert is committed before the project begins |
| The rules generated by the expert are short and simple, in that they do not provide a high degree of accuracy in complex situations | Avoid using "toy problems" – try to monitor the expert solving realistic problems. Use realistic data, for example lab tests etc., and vary the types of problem |
| The expert seems less and less enthusiastic about the project – the time he or she makes available declines over a period | Make sure that the knowledge engineer and expert meet on a regular basis (weekly at least). Involve the expert in building where possible, for example on-line testing and modification using "user-friendly" computer tools |
| The expert is unfamiliar with computers and is sceptical of the usefulness of an expert system | Gradually introduce the functionality of the expert system in the workplace. Prototyping can have value here with users becoming aware of the benefits of the expert system |
| So many experts are being used that the knowledge engineer does not have time to explore reasoning in depth | Try to avoid using too many experts initially. It is also important to build a good working relationship with the experts. Remember that the process of knowledge acquisition requires that the expert learns something about expert systems and the knowledge engineer learns something about the domain |

(b) What method(s) of knowledge elicitation would you prefer to use for this application domain and why? You do not necessarily have to choose any of the three methods described above in this question.

**8.** After reading a news report about expert systems, Professor Knowall has decided to build one. His plan is to build a voicewriter. That is, a knowledge-based typewriter that would print out whatever he says into a microphone. The voicewriter should also accept simple spoken commands to control word processing. His first step is to find some expert listeners and typists. Reasoning that secretaries sometimes have to take notes and then type letters and that a few of them can take dictation, he decides that they have the required knowledge. He solicits the aid of the secretaries of his department, to interview them about how they understand language and use a typewriter, and to acquire their knowledge by taking protocols of them doing this task.

(a) What knowledge does Professor Knowall need to access for representation of a voicewriter? Give your inventory in terms of the following skills:

- Typing skills
- Hearing skills
- Grammar, punctuation and articulation skills
- Word processing skills
- Document layout skills
- Critiquing skills

For each skill, say briefly what its knowledge elements are, whether the secretary has them, and whether or how it is relevant to building a voicewriter.

(b) Do the secretaries have this knowledge? If yes, would the knowledge be accessible using interviews and protocol analysis?

---

### *References and further reading*

Debenham, J. K. (1990) Knowledge engineering: the essential skills, in *Expert Systems for Management & Engineering*, Chichester: Ellis Horwood.

Edwards, J. S. (1990) *Building Knowledge Based Systems*, London: Pitman Press.

Feigenbaum, E. A. (1980) *Knowledge Engineering in the 1980's* Dept. of Computer Science, Stanford University, Stanford, CA.

Firlej, M. and Hellens, D. (1991) *Knowledge Elicitation – A Practical Handbook*, Hemel Hempstead: Prentice Hall.

Gaines, B. and Boose, J. (1988) *Knowledge Acquisition for Knowledge Based Systems*, London: Academic Press.

Hart, A. (1985) The role of induction in knowledge elicitation. *Expert Systems*, vol. 2, 24–28.

Hayes-Roth, F., Waterman, D. A. and Lenat, D. B. (1983) *Building Expert Systems*, Reading, MA: Addison-Wesley.

Kelly, G. (1955) *The Psychology of Personal Constructs*, New York: Norton.

Kidd, A. (1987) *Knowledge Acquisition for Expert Systems*, New York: Plenum Press.

McGraw, K. and Harbison-Briggs, K. (1990) *Knowledge Acquisition: Principles and Guidelines*, Hemel Hempstead: Prentice Hall.

Smith, P. (1996) *An Introduction to Knowledge Engineering*, London: ITCP.

CHAPTER 5

# Inference

**Objectives**

In this chapter you will learn:

- to understand the operation of the inference engine;
- to understand forward and backward chaining;
- to distinguish between deductive, inductive and abductive reasoning;
- to understand case-based reasoning (CBR);
- to understand shallow and deep reasoning;
- to appreciate the appropriateness of reasoning styles to various application domains.

## 5.1 Introduction

It was seen in Chapter 2 that the main components of an expert system are the inference engine, the knowledge base, and the user interface, which provides a means of communicating with an expert system. This chapter considers the inference component, and looks at a range of inference mechanisms that are used for constructing an expert system. Inference is important because it encompasses the techniques by which expert systems solve problems. The term *inference*, according to a dictionary definition, means: "to arrive at knowledge by reasoning." In rule-based systems, this means drawing conclusions from premises. This is achieved by the inference engine, and is now discussed in more detail.

## 5.2 The operation of the inference engine

In rule-based expert systems, the inference engine works by selecting a rule for testing and then checking if the conditions for that rule are true. The conditions may be found from questions to the user, or they may be facts already discovered during the consultation. When the conditions of the rule are found to be true, then the conclusion of the rule is true. The rule is then said to have "fired." The conclusion of this rule will then be added to the knowledge base or may be displayed via the user interface for information. For example, consider the following rules taken from a house plant adviser expert system:

RULE 1 *if* room is cool
and light is poor
then best plant is ivy;

RULE 2 *if* temperature <55
then room is cool;

If the inference engine was trying to prove the conclusion in RULE 1, then it would require values for the two conditions in this rule. That is, "room is cool" and "light is poor." The condition "room is cool" is found by trying to prove RULE 2 because it is a conclusion of this rule and thus would have to be found by evaluating this rule. This means that the conditions for RULE 2, that is "temperature <55", must be true. However, the condition "light is poor" would be found by asking the user for its value since it is not a conclusion of another rule and therefore its value can only be obtained by asking the user. In the above example, the inference engine could try to find the value for best plant by starting with RULE 1 and trying to prove the premises leading to the goal. Alternatively, the inference engine could have started from RULE 2 and then proceed forward to the problem solution.

### *Backward chaining*

Backward chaining starts from a conclusion, and tries to prove the conditions leading to that conclusion. This is a very common approach in diagnostic systems. Consider, for example, a car that will not start. This could be due to several causes, such as no petrol in the fuel tank, or a faulty starter motor, and so on. Humans frequently tackle this type of problem by starting from the suspected fault and checking the conditions that caused that fault to occur. As another more detailed example, consider the extract of rules taken from the healthcare expert system shown in Fig. 5.1. Assume the main goal of this system is to determine a patient's risk of heart failure. Consider what happens when this system tries to find a value for this goal, using backward-chaining inference.

Using backward chaining, the inference engine will search for the first rule in the knowledge base with heart failure in the conclusion. This is clearly RULE 1, that is risk of heart failure is high. To prove the conclusion in RULE 1, the inference engine needs to prove that the value given for the condition in this rule is true. That is, "blood pressure is likely to be high." This condition can only be found by trying to prove RULE 3 since it is a conclusion of this rule.

RULE 1 *if* blood pressure is likely to be high
then risk of heart failure is high

RULE 2 *if* blood pressure is likely to be low
then risk of heart failure is low

RULE 3 *if* alcoholic consumption is high
and patient salt intake is high
then blood pressure is likely to be high

RULE 4 *if* patient alcohol consumption is low
and patient salt intake is low
then patient blood pressure is likely to be low

RULE 5 *if* units of alcohol per week are >30
then patient alcohol consumption is high

RULE 6 *if* units of alcohol per week are <20
then patient alcohol consumption is low

RULE 7 *if* units of alcohol per week are >=20 and <=30
then patient alcohol consumption is average

QUESTION units of alcohol

QUESTION salt intake

FIND risk of heart failure

**Figure 5.1** Health promotion knowledge base

This means that the conditions for RULE 3, that is "alcoholic consumption is high", "patent salt intake is high", and so on, would need to be evaluated. To find a value for "alcoholic consumption is high", the condition in RULE 5 would have to be true, that is "units of alcohol per week are>30." A value for this condition would be found by asking the user a question. This is because it is not the conclusion of any rule in the knowledge base, and therefore its value can only be found by asking the user. The value for this condition would be found by asking the user to input the units of alcohol. If the user were to input a value for the units of alcohol >30, then RULE 5 would clearly succeed. The value "patient alcohol consumption is high" would then be used in RULE 3. Thus, the next condition in RULE 3, "patient salt intake is high", would be sought. Since this is not in a rule conclusion, the user would be asked for its value by a question. If the answer given by the user on the patient salt intake was "high", then RULE 3 would succeed and consequently RULE 1 would succeed. This process is called an *inference chain*. On the other hand, if the answer given by the user on the salt intake was low, then RULE 3 would fail. In this event, the inference engine would seek the next rule in the knowledge base with patient blood pressure in the conclusion. This is RULE 4. The inference engine would proceed to try to prove RULE 4 in the same way as it did in trying to prove RULE 3.

## 5.3 Inference strategies

Three inference strategies commonly used by experts are: deductive inference, inductive inference and abductive inference. These are now described in some detail.

### *Deductive inference*

Deductive inference was briefly considered in Chapter 2. The example took three propositions (1), (2) and (3), which were:

| | |
|---|---|
| Rachel is a programmer; | (1) |
| All programmers are happy, | (2) |
| therefore Rachel is happy. | (3) |

The conclusion (3) in this example is a logical consequence of, or can be deduced from, the premises (1) and (2). In this example, the conclusion can be inferred solely from the information given and is an example of deductive inference. Proposition (1) is called the *major premise*. Proposition (2) is called the *minor premise*. The deduction of (3) from (1) and (2) is a consequence of entailment as shown in the Venn diagram in Fig. 5.2.

The attraction of deductive inference is that it is a form of reasoning that is mathematically exact. This means that if the premises are true, then the conclusion is guaranteed also to be true.

### *Inductive inference*

Consider the following propositions:

| | |
|---|---|
| Minsky is a cat; | (4) |
| therefore Minsky has four legs. | (5) |

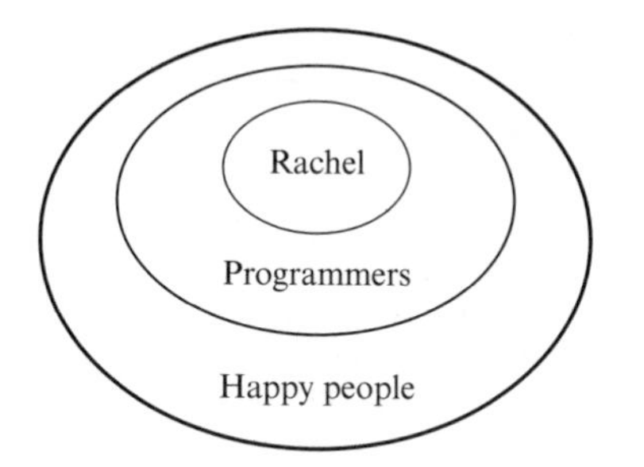


**Figure 5.2** Venn diagram illustrating entailment

On first inspection, it may be tempting to assume that the above conclusion (5), namely "Minsky has four legs", follows by deduction from the premise (4). However, this assumption is false for the premise (4) says nothing about whether or not a cat has four legs. Human beings would draw upon their own real-world knowledge about animals to assume this premise (that a cat has four legs) and arrive at the conclusion (5). Hence, the conclusion (5) does not have the same mathematical exactness that the previous conclusion (3) had. For the conclusion (5) to be true the assumption that "a cat has four legs" would have to be induced from human common-sense knowledge of the world and added to the given premise (4). For this reason, such inferences are called *inductive inferences*. Note that this is reasoning from specific to general in the sense that a cat is assumed to have four legs from observed experience of cats. This form of inference lacks the mathematical exactness of deduction – meaning that there is always the possibility that the conclusions are false. However, inductive inference is common in expert systems because it does match human inference in the real world.

### *Abductive inference*

Abductive inference explains effects in terms of their causes. This contrasts with deductive inference, which works from causes to effects. For example, consider the rule "if it is raining then the grass in the garden will get wet." The truth of the premise will ensure the truth of the conclusion. This is cause and effect. Abductive reasoning applied to this rule would assume the truth of the converse. That is, "if the grass in the garden is wet then it has been raining." This rule would be generally accepted even though there is no guarantee of its correctness. It is possible that the grass has become wet because it has been sprayed with water, or perhaps for some other reason. Thus, abductive reasoning also lacks the mathematical exactness of deductive reasoning. However, human experts frequently apply abductive inference. Table 5.1 summarises the main characteristics of each of these strategies.

Table 5.1 *Inference strategies*

| *Inference strategy* | *Characteristics* |
|---|---|
| Deductive reasoning | Requires and uses only the information given to solve problems<br>Reasoning from general to specific using the concept of entailment. The entailment relation means that if the premise is true then the conclusion must be true: that is, the conclusions are guaranteed true if premises are true |
| Inductive inference | Additional knowledge from experience required<br>Reasoning from specific to general. There is always the possibility that the conclusions are false |
| Abductive inference | Reasoning from effect to cause. There is, therefore, always the possibility that the conclusions are false |

## Self-assessment exercise

Are the following inferences abductive, deductive or inductive? Justify your answers.

(a) Nobody wins, therefore nobody should play.
(b) All birds can fly; all swallows are birds, therefore all swallows can fly.

## 5.4 Case-based reasoning

Case-based reasoning (CBR) works by selecting a case from a stored database of past cases that best resemble the characteristics of the problem currently under investigation. This is not dissimilar to the way in which human experts may reason when attempting to solve certain classes of problem. For example, a doctor deciding on a drug dosage level for a patient who is experiencing pain may be reminded of a similar patient experiencing similar pain a few weeks earlier. If the dosage level was acceptable and the circumstances were similar then it is quite likely that the decision made by the doctor is the same as was made previously. CBR is a method of inference fundamentally different from other approaches. Instead of relying on general knowledge of a problem domain, or making associations between problem premises and conclusions, CBR is able to utilise the specific knowledge of previously experienced, concrete problem situations. These are called *cases*. A new problem is solved by finding a similar past case and reusing it in the new problem situation. The case may be either reused to the solutions directly or, if necessary, adapted to the changed circumstances of the current problem. This is the approach that underpins the CBR method. A case is a description of a problem together with details of the action that would be taken to respond to the problem. The typical solution of a CBR problem would involve the following steps:

1. Record the details of the current problem.
2. Match these details against the details of stored cases to find similar problem situations.
3. Select the stored cases most relevant to the current problem.
4. Adapt the stored solution to the current problem.
5. Validate any new solution and store the details of the new case.

These problem-solving steps give rise to the problem-solving cycle of a typical CBR system, as illustrated in Fig. 5.3.

The four general processes shown in Fig. 5.3 are known as the four Rs. They are:

1. **Retrieve** the most similar case for inspection.
2. **Reuse** the information and knowledge in that case to solve the problem.
3. **Revise** the proposed solution.
4. **Retain** the parts of this experience likely to be used for future problem solving.

A new CBR problem is solved by retrieving one, or more, previously stored cases, reusing the case in the problem under consideration, revising the solution based on this reused case, and retaining the new case by incorporating it into the

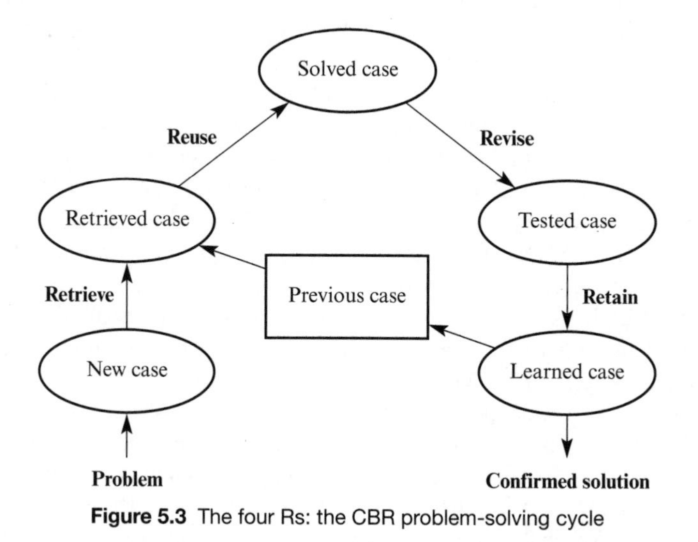


**Figure 5.3** The four Rs: the CBR problem-solving cycle

stored knowledge base of cases. Once a matching case is retrieved, a CBR system will attempt to reuse the solution suggested by the retrieved case. In some circumstances, the solution will not be sufficient. In such cases, the CBR system must adapt the solution stored in the retrieved case to the needs of the current case. Several methods have been used in CBR for adaptation (Watson 1997), some of which will be examined in the next section.

### *Applying CBR*

CBR (Cunningham 1998) can sometimes be effective in the following situations:

- Where experience, rather than theory, is the primary source of knowledge.
- Where solutions are reusable, rather than being unique to each situation.
- Where the objective is the best available solution rather than a guaranteed exact solution.

### *Applications of CBR*

Successful examples of CBR applications include help desk applications, diagnostic applications and training application domains. CBR is well suited to help desk applications because help desk knowledge is not easily underpinned by a theoretical understanding of the domain. For example, a computer-hardware retailing help desk uses knowledge about processors, peripherals, hard disks, and so on that is constantly changing, and therefore it is almost impossible to maintain a theoretical model of the domain.

An example of a diagnostic application of CBR is CASEY (Koton 1989). This is a healthcare CBR system that diagnoses cardiac patients on the basis of diagnoses of previous patients. CASEY makes use of some causal rules to guide the adaptation process. For example, CASEY can substitute its own knowledge that irregular heart rate suggests arteriosclerosis with a causal link between high blood pressure and arteriosclerosis. In this way, CASEY can adapt possible solutions to given cases. Another healthcare CBR application has been developed for AIDS prevention (Xu 1994). The epidemic has stimulated a variety of AIDS intervention and prevention (AIP) activities. Instead of serving those who are HIV positive, the purpose of AIP is to target individuals who exhibit high risk behaviour concerning hypodermic needle sharing, unsafe sex, and so on. One of the main operations in the AIP programme is called the AIDS Initial Assessment (AIA).

AIA is used to identify individuals at risk from AIDS. In AIA, experts extract the data from a database, and interpret that data with a view to selecting those likely to be at high risk. AIA is also concerned with the screening of AIDS-risky behaviours. CBR uses past cases to guide the problem-solving process. In AIA, generating an assessment from scratch is a time-consuming process, so CBR is used by experts to recall previous cases that are similar to any new case under investigation. If only part of the new case is addressed by previous cases then AIA experts may apply a modified version of the previous case to the new case. This means that new cases can be adapted to previous cases if they do not bear sufficient similarity. Adaptation in this system is essentially left to human experts.

### *CBR tools*

Many commercial CBR development tools are now available. These include ReCall written by ISoft[1], and CBR Express and Casepoint, both distributed by Inference Corporation[2]. Many CBR tools are capable of running on Pentium PCs under the Windows 98 operating system. Some CBR tools are application specific. For example, Casepoint is well suited to help desk applications. Figure 5.4 illustrates another tool from Inference Corporation called CBR Express. The illustration shows how this tool is being used to solve PC printer problems.

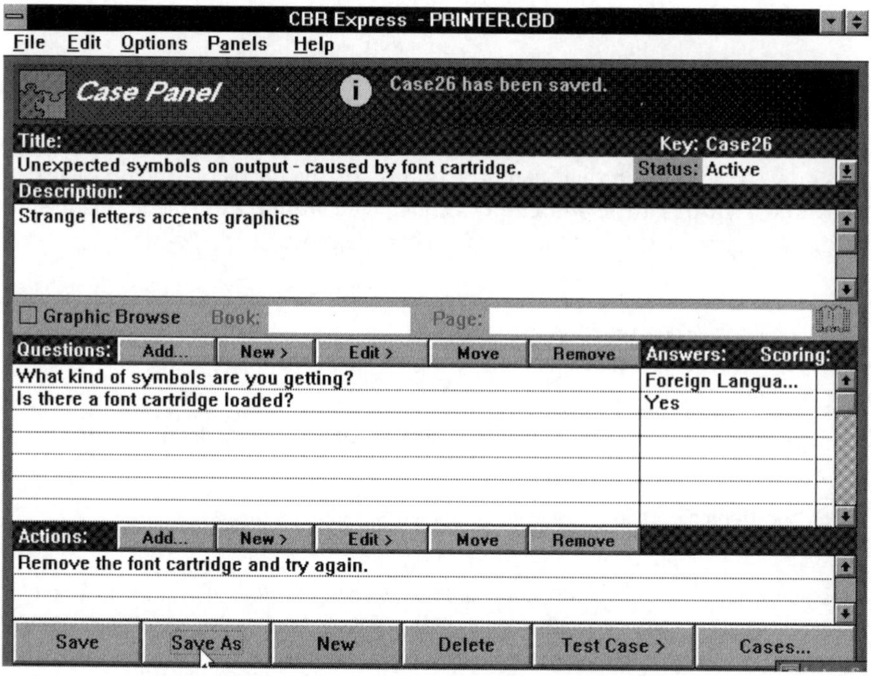

**Figure 5.4** Solving PC printer problems with CBR Express

---

[1] Isoft, Gif Sur Yvette, France (http://www.alice.fr).

[2] Inference Corporation, Slough, Berkshire (http://www.inference.co.uk).

## 5.5 CBR vs. traditional expert systems

In Chapter 2, it was seen that many expert systems store knowledge in the form of rules. As already seen, these rule-based systems attempt to solve problems by using a combination of rules in an appropriate chaining mechanism, usually forward or backward chaining. This approach relies on having access to the problem-solving knowledge, and knowledge of the application domain. The CBR approach, on the other hand, does not require knowledge of the domain, since CBR only needs to identify whether a similar previous problem has been solved. This gives the following advantages in applying CBR:

- Reduction in knowledge acquisition, since no explicit model of the workings of the domain is necessary.
- Enhanced maintenance capability because changes to domain knowledge can be updated with new solved cases.
- Learning capabilities by virtue of acquiring new cases over time without having to add new rules or modify existing rules.

Table 5.2 compares the traditional expert system approach with CBR.

## 5.6 Heuristic or shallow knowledge

Most expert systems use knowledge that is based on heuristics. Such knowledge is said to be shallow in that its representation of the problem domain is superficial and requires little understanding of the underlying mechanisms. For example, consider the rule taken from a car diagnostic expert system:

Table 5.2 *Conventional expert systems vs. CBR*

| | *Traditional expert systems* | *CBR* |
|---|---|---|
| Problem area | Narrow, well-understood model of domain | Weak domain model |
| Knowledge representation | If–then rules, frames, logic, etc. | Cases |
| Inference mechanism | Forward and backward chaining of rules, using defaults in frames, and so on | Selection of previous problem case closely resembling current problem characteristics |
| Learning capability | Very limited | Good. Achieved by case acquisition |

*if* car is consuming excessive fuel
*and* the_engine_is_misfiring = yes
*then* replace_spark_plugs = yes;

The rule above describes *shallow heuristic knowledge* in that the effect is not linked in terms of theoretically explainable premises, but practical and simple premises intended to achieve rapid results. This is explained further in the next section.

### Deep causal reasoning

Many researchers have demonstrated (Chandrasekaran, Tanner and Josephson 1988) the value of expert systems utilising reasoning from first principles. This is called *deep reasoning*. For example, an expert system advising on a strategy for maintaining an allotment of garden vegetables might include a rule such as:

*if* it rains,
*then* the vegetables will grow faster (1)

This rule, as it stands, is another example of *shallow reasoning*. It means that there is little or no understanding of cause and effect in shallow reasoning because there is no inference chain. This is an example of a heuristic in which all the knowledge is contained in the rule. A rule such as this may be regarded as a condensed form of a more complex explanation of some chemical phenomenon. However, the scientific cause of this rule could be broken down further into more detail such as:

*if* it rains *then* the vegetables will grow faster
*because* the soil will become more moist

This process of expansion could continue *ad nauseam*. Thus a deep causal model of the domain could be formulated by breaking down rule (1) into a deep causal chain. One of the immediate advantages of applying a deep model of the domain is that it provides better-quality explanations. A deep representation model of the domain can provide a deeper explanation of its behaviour because a deeper explicit model of the causal chain of reasoning will be available.

Chandrasekaran, Tanner and Josephson (1988) have applied deep models to provide explanations for justifying domain knowledge with much success. However, in many domains, deep knowledge is itself difficult to obtain and sometimes meaningless. For example, a program already being distributed by the British Medical Association (BMA) is an expert system that embodies the ethics and rules of law relating to "consent." That is, it clarifies the various issues involved in whether a particular patient is competent to give medical consent to treatment. Clearly, it is not possible to build a deep causal model of this type of domain, since the rules in this expert system would not be underpinned by any theoretical foundation. Nevertheless, the BMA has used this system as a training aid for nursing, paramedical and medical students. Southwick (1986) cites other examples in the legal domain where deep knowledge is not available.

## Exercises

1. Distinguish between searching and chaining.
2. Give two example domains of where you think case-based reasoning could be used.
3. What are the difficulties of implementing deep knowledge in an expert system?
4. List two application domains where you think abductive reasoning may be used.
5. Explain what is meant by reasoning from first principles. Give two advantages of building an expert system that uses reasoning from first principles.
6. Instead of providing a troubleshooting guide in a user manual, a printer manufacturer is considering building a CBR help desk expert system to enable customers to solve basic categories of printer problems on their own. The manufacturer intends to supply a disk containing the help desk system with each printer sold. Give three possible benefits of such a system for (a) the manufacturer and (b) the customer.
7. Why is it difficult to implement help desk applications using rule-based expert systems?

## *References and further reading*

Chandrasekaran, B., Tanner, M. C. and Josephson, J. R. (1988) Explanation: the role of control strategies and deep models. In *Expert Systems: The User Interface*, Norwood, NJ: Ablex.

Cunningham, P. (1998) *11th IEA Conference*, Berlin: Springer.

Darlington, K. (1997) Expert systems in nursing. *British Computer Society ITIN*, vol. 9.2.

Durkin, J. (1994) *Expert Systems: Design and Development*, London: Macmillan.

Dutta, S. (1995) *Knowledge Processing and Applied AI*, Oxford: Butterworth-Heinemann.

Giarratano, J. C. and Riley, G. D. (1994) *Expert Systems: Principles and Programming*, 2nd edition, Boston: PWS Kent.

Jackson, P. (1992) *Introduction to expert systems*, Addison-Wesley.

Koton, P. (1989) Using experiences in learning and problem solving. PhD Thesis, MIT.

Southwick, R. (1986) Topic explanations in expert systems. *BCS Proceedings of UK Expert Systems Conference*.

Watson, I. (1997) *Applying CBR*, San Francisco: Morgan Kaufmann.

Xu, L. D. (1994) Developing a CBR knowledge system for AIDS prevention. *Expert System User*, vol. 11, no. 4.

CHAPTER 6

# *Software for building expert systems*

**Objectives**

In this chapter you will learn:

- to appreciate the appropriateness of different software tools for building expert systems;
- to understand the characteristics of AI languages;
- to understand the characteristics of expert system shells;
- to understand the characteristics of AI toolkits;
- to be aware of building aids for knowledge acquisition;
- to apply criteria in order to select an appropriate expert system development tool.

## 6.1 Introduction

The term *expert system tools* loosely describes the software that is used for constructing an expert system. These tools range from programs that are used for building the expert system to programs that can aid the knowledge acquisition process. Figure 6.1 describes the relationship between the general categories of expert system tools.

## 6.2 Tools for developing expert systems

The main software tools for developing expert systems fall into the following categories:

- Programming languages
- Expert system shells
- AI toolkits

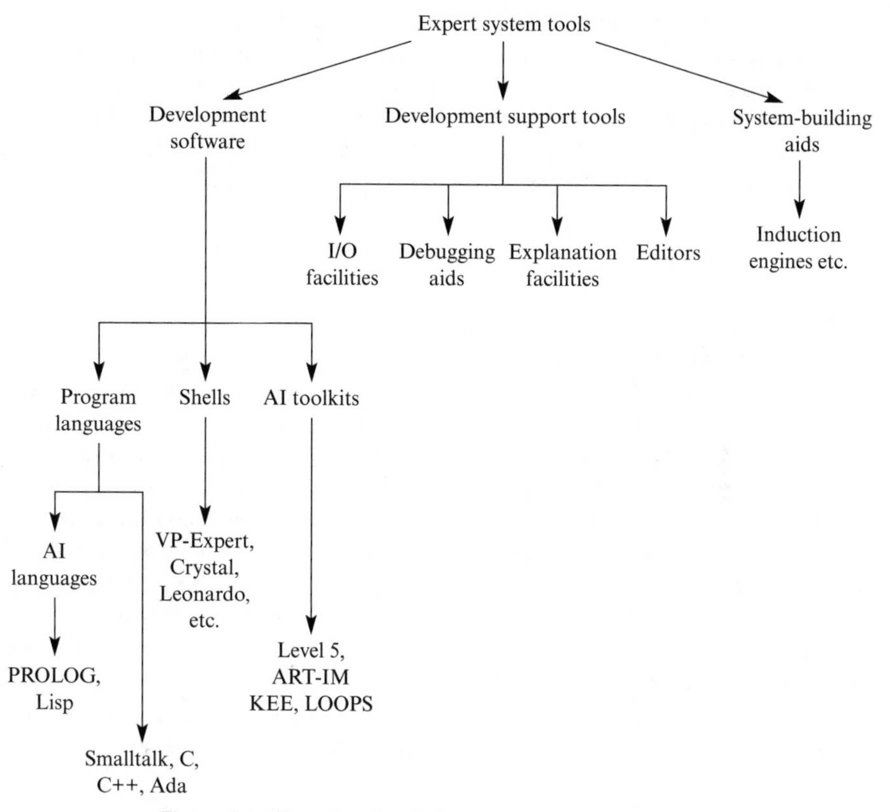


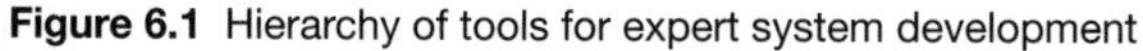

**Figure 6.1** Hierarchy of tools for expert system development

## 6.3 Programming languages

The languages used for developing expert systems fall into two general categories:

1. Conventional languages
2. AI languages

### *Conventional languages*

Conventional languages are also called problem-oriented languages. Examples are *C*, *COBOL*, *Smalltalk* and *Ada*. One of the main benefits of using conventional languages is the availability of interfaces to conventional software, such as databases or spreadsheets. However, many of the specific expert system development tools now commercially available also have these facilities (see Section 9.4). It is possible to build an expert system using a conventional programming language like C or Pascal, or even COBOL, just as it is possible to cut a lawn with scissors! But these languages are unsuitable for building expert systems because they are not suited for manipulating the structures for which knowledge is represented. COBOL, for example, was designed for data processing and not the representation and control of knowledge. Nevertheless, expert systems have been built using languages like C, whose main advantage is its speed of compilation.

### *AI languages*

AI languages are also called *symbol-manipulation languages* because they have been designed for AI applications. The most common examples are Lisp and PROLOG. The first batch of expert systems were mostly developed using Lisp. Building expert systems with high-level languages can be very time consuming, frequently taking several years, because the builder has to develop the user interface from scratch and implement the inference engine using the structures available in the language. An example of one such system was DENDRAL, a chemical analysis expert system that was used to infer the molecular structure of unknown compounds from mass spectral data. PROSPECTOR is an example of a mineral exploitation expert system that acts as a consultant to aid exploration geologists in their search for mineral deposits. Another example is XCON, the computer company DEC's configuration system. From a customer's order it decides what components must be added to produce a

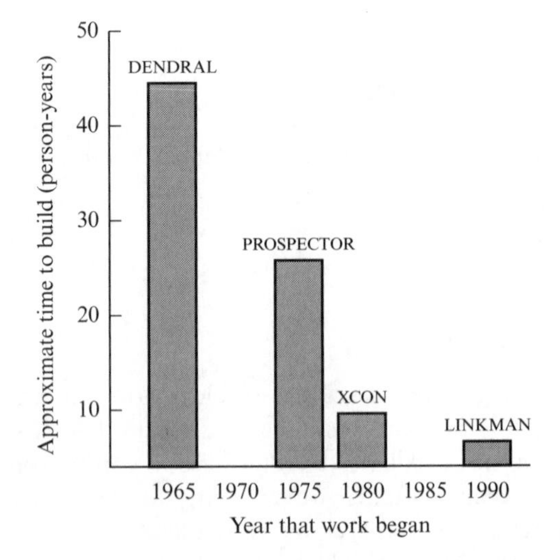


**Figure 6.2** Development times of expert systems

complete operational system from the specification of the order. Figure 6.2 shows the approximate development time for each of these three systems, along with the LINKMAN expert system, which was developed in 1990. The figure clearly shows that expert system development time has been vastly reduced over the last 30 years, particularly in the last 10 years. This is mainly due to improvements in development tools. The most common tools now being used for expert system development are called *expert system shells*.

## 6.4 Expert system shells

Shells provide an easy starting point for building an expert system because of their ease of use. They are expert systems that have been emptied of their rules. This means that developers can concentrate on entering the knowledge base without having to build everything, including the inference engine and user interface, from scratch. Even non-programming experts can familiarise themselves with shells fairly rapidly. Also, many expert system shells contain facilities that can simplify knowledge acquisition (see next section). Non-programming experts can acquire an understanding of shells without undertaking the lengthy learning process that programming other types of software development requires.

However, using a shell to build an expert system can seduce the builder into oversimplifying the application domain because shells are inflexible, in that it is difficult to modify or change the way they work with regard to both representation of knowledge and the inference mechanism. It is therefore important not to let the shell dictate the representation of the domain, for the result will be reflected in the performance of the system. There are several shells commercially available. These include: AM for Windows 95, previously known as Crystal, Leonardo and EXSYS. They all operate on PC-compatible hardware using Windows. An illustration of the Leonardo development environment is given in Fig. 6.3.

### *Domain-specific shells*

Several tools are now available for developing specific application domains. For example, there exist shells for diagnostic systems, shells for configuration systems, scheduling systems, help desk systems, and so on. Domain-specific shells enhance the more general shells by providing special development support and a user interface. An example of a domain-specific tool was mentioned in the last chapter, namely CBR Express, a CBR tool specifically suited to help desk applications. Domain-specific shells tend to be more expensive than general-purpose shells (Price 1990).

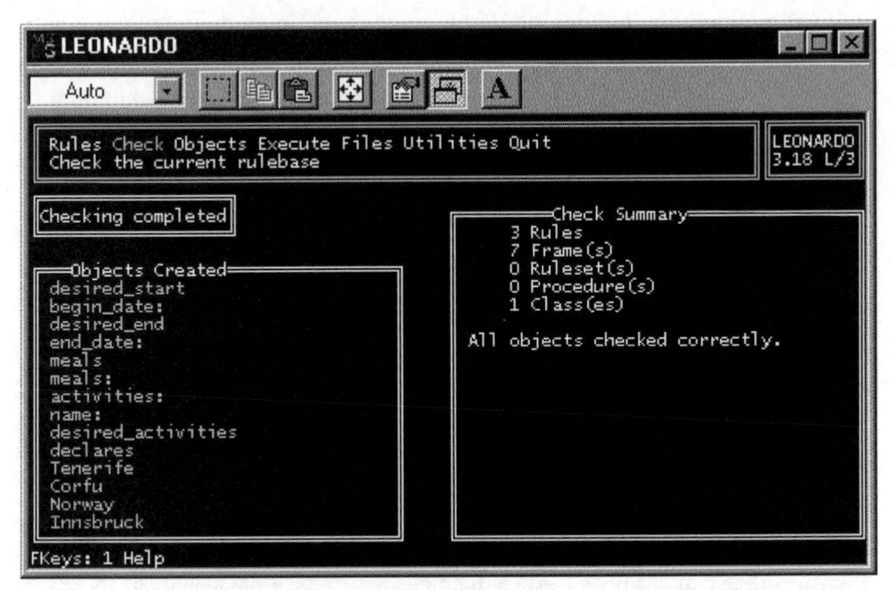


**Fig. 6.3** Illustration of the Leonardo expert system shell environment

### *CBR development shells*

A range of special-purpose shells are available for CBR. Harmon (1992) has reviewed four such shells. These are ReMind from Cognitive Systems Inc., CBR Express /ART-IM from Inference Corp., Esteem from Esteem Software Inc., and CasePower from Inductive Solutions.

## 6.5 AI toolkits

Other tools for building expert systems are called *AI toolkits* or *environments*. These are very sophisticated "hybrid tools", which typically contain code structures for a range of expert system tasks. They make use of rules, frames, object-oriented programming (OOP), and logic or semantic networks. They may also use forward and backward chaining, CBR, and a wide variety of inheritance techniques. AI toolkits are more specialised than shells. Therefore, they can increase productivity. However, because of their complexity, AI toolkits require more skill than shells or programming languages. Unlike shells, which are predominantly suited to small standalone applications, AI toolkits are more suited to larger client/server corporate applications. Two of the most commonly used AI toolkits (Laurent *et al.* 1989) are:

1. ART-IM is a comprehensive PC Lisp-based toolkit available in DOS and Windows versions. It has four main component rules (used mainly for procedural knowledge), facts, schemata (frames) and viewpoints (for declarative knowledge). ART is well suited to complex applications, and especially real-time applications such as intelligent interpretation of sensor data from a factory floor.
2. Level 5 Object is a PC-based toolkit that is well suited to client/server applications. It has built-in interfaces to all the common and remote database servers. As with ART-IM, Level 5 Object supports a variety of formalisms for representing knowledge, including rules, frames, and demons. It is also supported with extensive reasoning capabilities. The development environment (Bielawski and Lewand 1991) includes a *rule editor*, *objects editor* and *display editor* for designing the user interface in a Windows environment. The rule editor interacts with the developer to keep track of rules within the system, displays and knowledge trees. Knowledge trees offer a visual means of graphically displaying a knowledge base as a decision tree. The object editor allows the developer the means of creating and editing object classes (see Fig. 6.4). The display editor gives the developer full control over check boxes, radio buttons, text windows, hyper-regions, and more Windows development tools.

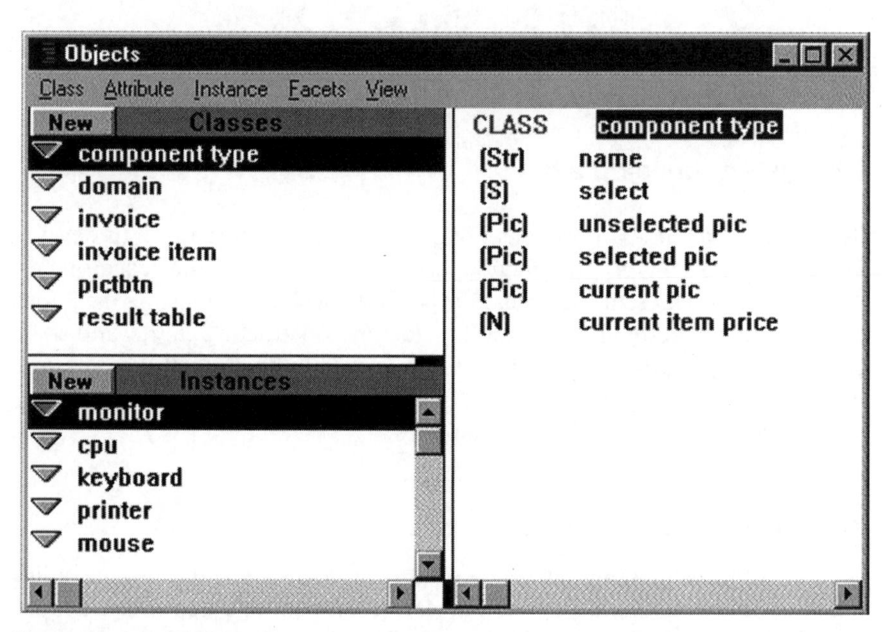


**Figure 6.4** Level 5 Object illustrating object hierarchies (courtesy of Information Builders Inc.)

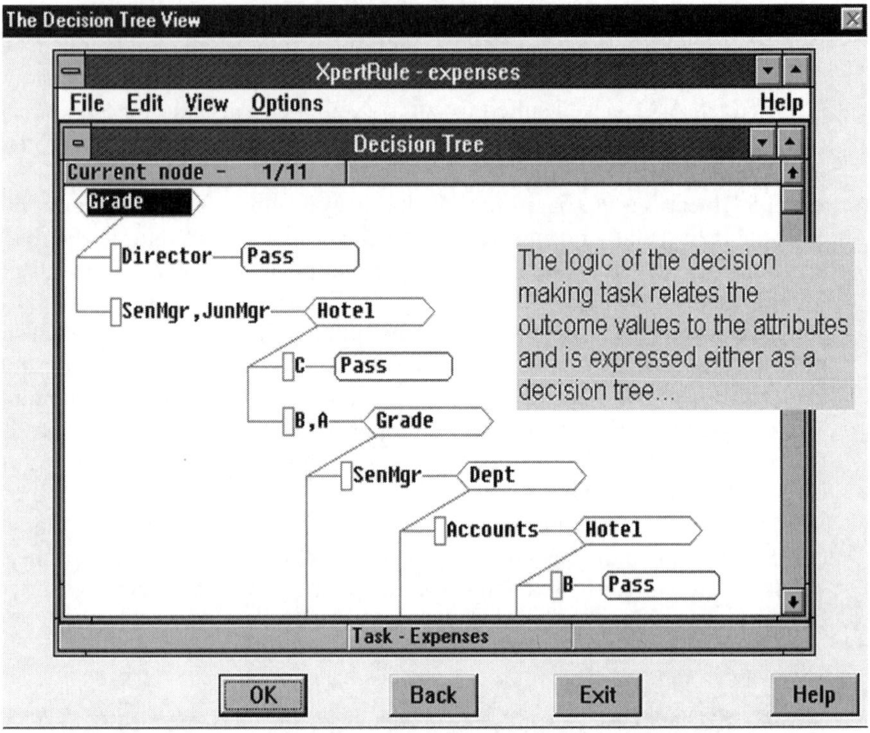

**Figure 6.5** Illustration of expert-system-building aids (courtesy of Attar Software)

## 6.6 System-building aids

System-building aids are various programs that support the overall development process. They range in functionality from helping the knowledge engineer to acquire and represent the domain expert's knowledge to assisting the knowledge engineer in designing the expert system by constructing charts, and so on. Commercially available system-building aids include *XpertRule* written by Attar Software. Figure 6.5 shows a typical display illustrating system-building aids that are used to generate decision trees.

### *Knowledge acquisition tools*

Manual methods of knowledge acquisition are expensive and time consuming. Much effort has gone into developing tools that facilitate knowledge acquisition. An "induction engine" is amongst the most commonly used, and is capable of inducing rules from given examples (Hart 1989). Though not an essential

Table 6.1 *Examples taken from a life assurance expert*

| *Example* | *Age* | *Smoker?* | *Gender* | *Risk* |
|---|---|---|---|---|
| 1 | Young | No | Female | Low |
| 2 | Old | Yes | Male | High |
| 3 | Middle | No | Male | Low |

part of an expert system, an induction engine is a useful adjunct provided with many expert system shells. The induction engine reads a set of examples, perhaps provided by the domain expert describing relationships between domain concepts. The inference engine will then attempt to produce the rules that link those examples together and then place them in the knowledge base. The examples are often depicted in tabular form. As an illustration, Table 6.1 shows three cases obtained from an expert in life insurance. The table examples show the dependence of a client's risk of death upon the factors shown.

The induction engine could "induce" the rules shown in Fig. 6.5 from the examples given in Table 6.1. It should be noted that there would not necessarily be a one-to-one correspondence between the number of examples in the table and the rules generated – that would depend upon the values that the different factors take.

The rules in Fig. 6.5 show how the induction technique generates general rules from specific examples.

RULE 1 *if* age is old
*and* gender is male
*and* smoker is yes
*then* risk is high;

RULE 2 *if* age is middle
*and* gender is male
*and* smoker is no
*then* risk is low;

RULE 3 *if* age is young
*and* gender is female
*and* smoker is no
*then* risk is low;

**Figure 6.6** Rules induced from examples

## 6.7 Choosing development tools

Selecting appropriate tools for building expert systems is more difficult than with conventional systems for, unlike the latter, many tools are not specifically suited to particular classes of problem. Building expert systems is generally considered to be an iterative process. This applies to the choice of tool, for very often the tool selected for the initial prototype may have to be changed later as part of the iterative process. This could be due to the following reasons:

- The builder was not aware of the limitations of the selected tool.
- Some important factors may have been overlooked during the requirement analysis.
- A tool was selected for prototyping with the intention of changing it, if necessary, when developing the full system.

The first reason is particularly important, because the speed of execution of an expert system will generally get slower as the knowledge base gets larger. Thus, if speed was an important factor in determining the choice of tool, the likely size of the expert system will need to be considered to determine to what extent it will affect the execution speed of the deliverable system. There are many questions that should be answered when selecting a tool, such as the following:

- Does the tool have the features suggested by the needs of the problem or application? For example, if the problem domain involves reasoning with uncertainty, does the tool have features for handling uncertainty, such as capabilities for manipulating certainty factors or Bayesian inference?
- Are the tool's support facilities adequate to ensure that the product can be tested and completed within the scheduled project time? For example, does the tool have facilities for testing, debugging, and so on? Figure 6.7 describes the components of the development support environment of a typical shell.

### *Evaluating expert system shells*

The following general criteria should be considered when selecting an appropriate shell for expert system development.

#### *Ease of use*

The adopted choice should be both easy to use and suited to rapid prototyping.

#### *Technical capabilities*

Shells vary greatly in the way that they represent knowledge and the way in which they apply inference strategies. Some shells, for example VP-Expert, are

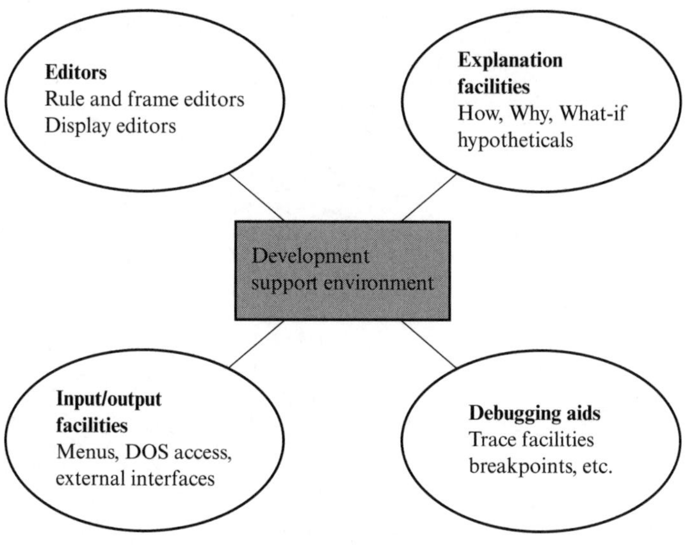


**Figure 6.7** Development support environment

strictly rule based. Others, such as Leonardo, support frame or object representations. The technical capabilities are an issue that will need to be addressed when the nature of the application domain is well understood by the developer.

### *Development support environment*

An expert system shell support environment should as a minimum include a built-in editor for entering the knowledge base code, debugging and tracing tools, and an interface to the explanation facilities.

### *User interface issues*

Shells should include tools for developing a quality user interface so that supportive, consistent and clear screens can be designed for the user during run-time, as well as facilities for navigation such as hypertext inclusion and Web page access.

### *External interfacing*

Most expert system projects require some degree of interfacing to external systems, such as spreadsheet files, databases, or even C++ routines. For example, a medical expert system might need to access patient data that is stored on a database. Clearly, an ability to integrate external programs and data is an essential prerequisite for the choice of many expert system tools.

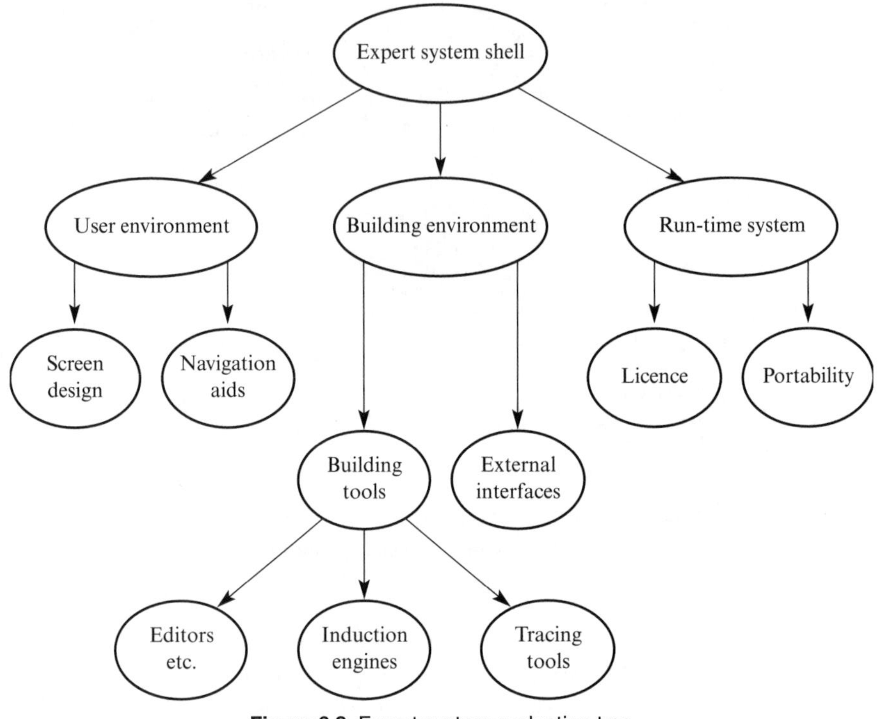


**Figure 6.8** Expert system evaluation tree

*Run-time licence and vendor support*

The run-time licence is another issue to be addressed when considering whether or not to use a particular shell. The run-time environment will determine how the developed product will be deployed as a standalone application. Some vendors include a free run-time licence, which means that applications can be developed and distributed without incurring additional costs. Other run-time licences may cost depending on the policy of the vendor.

Another factor that is related to the run-time environment is the portability of the product to other hardware/software platforms. For example, an expert system developed on a Pentium II PC running Windows 98 may not run on an older 486 PC running under DOS/Windows 3.11.

The tree diagram in Fig. 6.8 summarises the way the above evaluation issues relate to each other.

## 6.8 Conclusions

This chapter has examined a range of tools for expert system development.

Expert system shells provide a rapid means of familiarisation with the technology and are generally inexpensive. However, the limited single representation schemes available with shells would prevent the encoding of the knowledge in a realistic form for more complex systems. For a working model to behave like an expert, the expertise cannot be forced into the model of the representation scheme of the shell. However, despite their limitations, shells are used by many organisations. In some cases they are used at the start of the prototyping cycle in order to gain a better understanding of the problem requirements and are then discarded at a later stage. The following rule best summarises the choice of a tool for developing an expert system:

> *Use a shell if you can, a toolkit where you should, and an AI language when you must.*

---

## Exercises

1. Search the Internet and the World Wide Web to find out what you can about the knowledge acquisition tool called ACQUIST.
2. What support facilities would you expect to find in an expert system tool? What debugging facilities would you expect to find?
3. What are the advantages of using knowledge acquisition tools for:
   (a) the knowledge engineer
   (b) the expert?
4. A small advisory system is to be developed for a mobile phone company to assist telephone staff in troubleshooting mobile phone faults. Write a short report justifying the use of an expert system shell for the development of this system.

---

### *References and further reading*

Bielawski, L. and Lewand, R. (1991) *Intelligent System Design*, New York: John Wiley.
Black, W. (1986) *Intelligent Knowledge Based Systems*, Wokingham: Van Nostrand Reinhold.
Harmon, P. (1992) Case-based reasoning III. *Intelligent Software Strategies*, vol. 8, no.1.
Harmon, P. *et al.* (1988) *Expert Systems: Tools and Applications*, New York: John Wiley.
Hart, A. (1989) *Knowledge Acquisition for Expert Systems*, New York: McGraw-Hill.
Laurent, J. P., Ayel, J., Thome, F. and Zeibelin, D. (1989) Comparative evaluation of three expert system development tools. *KE Review*, vol. 1, no. 4.
Price, C. J. (1990) *Knowledge Engineering Toolkits*, Hemel Hempstead: Prentice Hall.

CHAPTER 7

# Uncertainty

**Objectives**

In this chapter you will learn:

- to understand why uncertainty needs to be represented in some expert systems;
- to distinguish between numerical and logical methods of handling uncertainty;
- to understand the methods of manipulating Bayes' and certainty factors;
- to know when to apply different numerical methods for use in expert systems;
- to build a simple model using Bayes' and certainty factors for representing uncertainty.

## 7.1 Introduction

In the previous chapters, facts have always been assumed to be either true or false. Unfortunately, such assumptions cannot be made with regard to many application domains. For example, a medical expert who is carrying out a patient diagnosis may need to know if the patient had measles when the patient was very young. The patient may not remember the answer to this question, and thus the expert may not have all this patient's information available to ensure a correct diagnosis. This means that the medical expert will frequently have to make a decision based on incomplete or uncertain data. Clearly, this may result in uncertain conclusions. Moreover, when a condition in a rule is known to be a certain value, the conclusion of the rule may not be known with certainty. For example, consider the rule:

*if* the car will not start
    *then* the battery is faulty (1)

The conclusion of the rule (1) may be true in some cases, but sometimes the conclusion will be false. There could be other causes of the problem such as a faulty starter motor, no petrol in the fuel tank, and so on. There are, therefore, two reasons why it might be necessary to use reasoning with uncertainty. They are:

1. The user may be uncertain of an answer to a question.
2. The conclusion of a rule may not always be guaranteed to be true, even if the premises of the rule are true.

Techniques for handling uncertainty fall into two categories: numerical and logical methods. Most practical expert systems use numerical methods. Some of these methods are based on the theory of probability. This theory assigns numerical values on a scale from 0 to 1 to the chances of an event occurring. The value 0 denotes the impossibility of an event occurring whilst the value 1 denotes the certainty of an event occurring. For example, if an event is considered as a card being randomly chosen from a normal pack of 52, then the probability of selecting a card numbered 14 is 0. This is because there is no card numbered 14 in an ordinary pack and, hence, such an event is impossible. On the other hand, the probability of selecting a card from the suits hearts, clubs, diamonds or spades is clearly 1, since any card in the pack has to be one of these suits and hence such an event is certain to occur.

There are a variety of probabilistic techniques used for representing uncertainty. One very successful technique is called Bayesian inference.

## 7.2 Bayesian inference

This method represents uncertainty by describing a model of the application domain as a set of possible outcomes known as the *hypothesis* (Giarratano and Riley 1992). For example, consider a medical expert who is attempting to diagnose a patient illness. The Bayesian approach would, perhaps, treat each patient illness such as influenza, bronchitis, and so on as the possible hypotheses in the problem space. Each hypothesis will clearly have an initial probability of occurring (even if it may be difficult to find).

The Bayesian method of inference requires an initial estimate of the probability for each of the possible hypotheses in the problem space. This is called a *prior* probability and must be known, or estimated, in advance. When prior probabilities are known, Bayesian inference then updates hypotheses by using the answers to questions supplied by the user during the running of the system. These may be questions such as "what is the body temperature of the patient?", "is the patient suffering from dizziness?", and so on. This is known as *evidence*. Each item of evidence will update the probability of each of the hypotheses being considered. These represent revised beliefs in the light of this known evidence and are then mathematically calculated from Bayes' theorem using the following formula:

$$P(H_i/E) = P(EH_i) \times P(H_i)/[\sum_{i=1}^{n} P(E/H_i) \times P(H_i)] \qquad (7.1)$$

where $P(H_i/E)$ is the probability that hypothesis $H_i$ is true, given evidence $E$; $P(E/H_i)$ is the probability that we will observe evidence $E$, given that $H_i$ is true; $P(H_i)$ is called the *prior* probability that hypothesis $i$ is true in the absence of any evidence; and $n$ is the number of possible hypotheses.

***Proof:*** From elementary probability theory

$$P(H_i/E) \times P(E) = P(E/H_i) \times P(H_i)$$

Hence:

$$P(H_i/E) = P(E/H) \times P(H_i)/P(E)$$

But:

$$P(E) = \Sigma\, P(E/H_i) \times P(H_i)$$

and therefore (7.1) follows.

**Example**

Suppose that there are four coins in a jar, and that each coin is either a 1p or 5p coin. Suppose also that there is at least one of each present in the jar. It is required to make inferences about the actual composition of coins in the jar, by selecting one coin taken from the jar at random.

**Solution**

Prior to any selection being made, it can be deduced that there are three possible hypotheses. They are:

$H_1$ consists of one 1p coin and three 5p coins.
$H_2$ consists of two 1p coins and two 5p coins.
$H_3$ consists of three 1p coins and one 5p coin.

These hypotheses are mutually exclusive and exhaustive, since none of them can occur together. The probability of each hypothesis is the same since they all have an equally likely chance of being selected. Thus, the probability of each hypothesis is 1/3, and is written as:

$$P(H_1) = P(H_2) = P(H_3) = 1/3$$

Suppose a coin is selected at random from the jar, and it turns out to be a 5p coin. How would this event change the probabilities of the hypotheses? The observed event, that a 5p coin is selected, is called *evidence* and is denoted by $E$.

We can find the conditional probability of $E$ occurring given $H_1$ since if this hypothesis is true then there are three 5p coins in the jar. Hence:

$$P(E/H_1) = 3/4$$

Similarly, if $H_2$ is true, then $P(E/H_2) = 2/4 = 1/2$. Also, if $H_3$ is true then $P(E/H_3) = 1/4$. Applying Bayes' theorem gives:

$$P(H_1/E) = P(E/H_1) \times P(H_1)/[\Sigma P(E/H_i) \times P(H_i)]$$

Inserting the numeric values into this formula gives:

$$\begin{aligned} P(H_1/E) &= (3/4 \times 1/3)/[3/4 \times 1/3 + 2/4 \times 1/3 + 1/4 \times 1/3] \\ &= (3/4)/(6/4) = \underline{1/2 \text{ answer}} \end{aligned}$$

This means that the probability of the hypothesis $H_1$ has increased from 1/3 to 1/2 as a result of observing the 5p coin. The probability of the hypothesis $H_2$ can be found in the same way. That is:

$$\begin{aligned} P(H_2/E) &= P(E/H_2) \times P(H_2)/[\Sigma P(E/H_i) \times P(H_i)] \\ &= (2/4 \times 1/3)/[3/4 \times 1/3 + 2/4 \times 1/3 + 1/4 \times 1/3] \\ &= \underline{1/3 \text{ answer}} \end{aligned}$$

Similarly, the conditional probability, given the 5p coin, for $H_3$ is:

$$\begin{aligned} P(H_3/E) &= P(E/H_3) \times P(H_3)/[\Sigma\, P(E/H_i) \times P(H_i)] \\ &= (1/4 \times 1/3)/[3/4 \times 1/3 + 2/4 \times 1/3 + 1/4 \times 1/3] \\ &= \underline{1/6 \text{ answer}} \end{aligned}$$

### *An alternative form of Bayes' theorem*

Bayes' theorem can also be written in an alternative form as shown below:

$$P(H/E) = P(E/H) \times P(H)/[P(E/H) \times P(H) + P(E/{\sim}H) \times P({\sim}H)] \qquad (7.2)$$

where $E$ denotes evidence as before, $H$ is some hypothesis under investigation, and $\sim H$ is the negated hypothesis.

**Example**

The prior probability that a patient at a hospital has bronchitis is 0.1. The probability that a patient who has a fever given that the patient has bronchitis is 0.9, and the probability that a patient has a fever given that the patient does not have bronchitis is 0.07. Find the probability that a patient with a fever has bronchitis.

**Solution**

The hypothesis $H$ is used to denote the patient's having bronchitis. The other hypothesis given here is the complement of $H$: that is, the patient not having bronchitis. This is written as $\sim H$. We use Bayes' theorem in the restated form (7.2). That is:

$$P(H/E) = P(E/H) \times P(H)/[P(E/H) \times \mathrm{P(H)} + P(E/\sim H) \times P(\sim H)] \qquad (7.2)$$

where $E$ is the evidence that the patient has fever, $H$ is the hypothesis that the patient has bronchitis, and $\sim H$ is the negated hypothesis, for example the patient does not have bronchitis.

Now, $P(H) = 0.1$ (given). Also, $P(E/H) = 0.9$ (given) and $P(E/\sim H) = 0.07$ (given). Hence, using Bayes' theorem in the form (7.2) and inserting the probabilities above:

$$P(H/E) = 0.9 \times 0.1/[0.9 \times 0.1 + 0.07 \times 0.1]$$
$$= \underline{0.93 \text{ answer}} \text{ (correct to two decimal places)}$$

As would be expected, the hypothesis that the patient has bronchitis has increased in the light of the evidence that the patient has a fever.

### *The odds-likelihood form*

In many expert system applications, developers often use a variation of Bayes' theorem called the odds-likelihood form. The odds-likelihood form is written as:

$$O(H) = P(H)/P(\sim H) = P(H)/[1 - P(H)]$$

or:

$$O(H/E) = P(H/E)/(P(\sim H/E) = P(H/E)/[1 - \mathrm{P}(H/E)]$$

where $O(H)$ represents the odds of $H$ occurring.

### Logical sufficiency

The logical sufficiency (LS) represents the measure of support for a hypothesis $H$ given that evidence $E$ is present. LS is calculated from the following formula:

$$\text{LS} = P(E/H)/P(E/{\sim}H) \tag{7.3}$$

Also:

$$P(H/E) = P(E/H) \times P(H)/P(E) \tag{7.4}$$

and:

$$P({\sim}H/E) = P(E/{\sim}H) \times P({\sim}H)/P(E) \tag{7.5}$$

From equations (7.1) to (7.5) above:

$$O(H/E) = P(H/E)/P({\sim}H/E)$$

Using (7.4) and (7.5) in the above for $P(H/E)$ and $P({\sim}H/E)$ gives:

$$O(H/E) = [P(E/H) \times P(H)/P(E)] \,/\, [P(E/{\sim}H) \times P({\sim}H)/\mathrm{P}(E)]$$

This can be rearranged to give:

$$\begin{aligned} O(H/E) &= [P(E/H)/P(E/{\sim}H)] \times [P(H)/P({\sim}H)] \\ &= \text{LS} \times O(H) \end{aligned}$$

Hence:

$$\text{LS} = O(H/E)/O(H) \tag{7.6}$$

This is called the *odds-likelihood form* and determines by what factor the odds of the hypothesis have increased, given that the evidence is true.

### Logical necessity

The logical necessity (LN) represents the measure of support for a hypothesis $H$ given that evidence $E$ is absent. LN is calculated from the following formula:

$$\text{LN} = P({\sim}E/H)/P({\sim}E/{\sim}H) = O(H/{\sim}E)/O(H)$$

Table 7.1 *The effect of boundary values of LS on H*

| *LS* | *Effect on hypothesis* |
|---|---|
| 0 | *H* is false when *E* is true |
| ∞ | The truth of *E* ensures the truth of *H* |
| 1 | The truth of *E* has no effect on *H* |

Table 7.2 *The effect of boundary values of LN on H*

| *LN* | *Effect on hypothesis* |
|---|---|
| 0 | *H* is true when *E* is false |
| ∞ | The truth of *E* ensures the truth of *H* |
| 1 | The truth of *E* has no effect on *H* |

or:

$$O(H/{\sim}E) = LN \times O(H) \tag{7.7}$$

This is called the *logical necessity form* and tells us by what factor the odds of the hypothesis have decreased, given that the evidence is false.

If LN = 0, then $P(H/{\sim}E) = 0$. This means that *H* must be false when ~*E* is true. If *E* is not present, then *H* is false, which means that *E* is necessary for *H*. Table 7.1 summarises the effect of boundary values of LS on *H*.

Similarly, Table 7.2 summarises the effect of boundary values of LN on hypothesis *H*.

Bayesian updating of hypotheses has been used with a great deal of success in some practical systems. Amongst the best known of these is PROSPECTOR (Duda *et al.* 1979). This expert system was briefly described in Chapter 6, and has been highly successful at locating mineral deposits such as copper and uranium.

## 7.3 Building expert systems using Bayesian inference

When using Bayesian inference to model uncertainty in expert systems, the odds-likelihood form is easier to apply than the probability formula described earlier in the chapter. The following example will illustrate how this technique is used in practice using the Leonardo expert system shell. Leonardo is a shell that has facilities for representing Bayesian inference and uses other methods for handling uncertainty. It is not necessary to have access to Leonardo to implement Bayesian inference. However, whatever expert system tool is used, the knowledge engineer will need to obtain prior probabilities for each hypothesis under consideration, and values of LS and LN for every piece of evidence that is used in the Bayesian model.

> **Example**
> This example uses a Bayesian model for the following assessment problem. An electronics retailer has to decide whether or not to stock a product line. The decision will depend on several factors, but for simplicity, assume that the decision depends solely on the factors of market size, total purchase cost and profit margin.
>
> This relationship is illustrated diagrammatically in Fig. 7.1.

In Leonardo terminology, *Buy* is the goal hypothesis, and *Market*, *Cost* and *Profit* are called antecedents.

### *The Bayesian hypothesis*

Any Bayesian problem has to consider hypotheses describing the problem space. When the hypotheses have been established, prior probabilities then have to be found for each hypothesis. In this example, assume there is only one goal hypothesis. The goal hypothesis in this example is Buy. A prior probability is just the probability of the goal's being true without knowing the status of its antecedents. For instance, if from past experience of other product lines the retailer knows that 1 in 5 of all new products turns out to be worth stocking, then the a priori probability of Buy would be 0.2. This is written as:

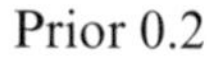


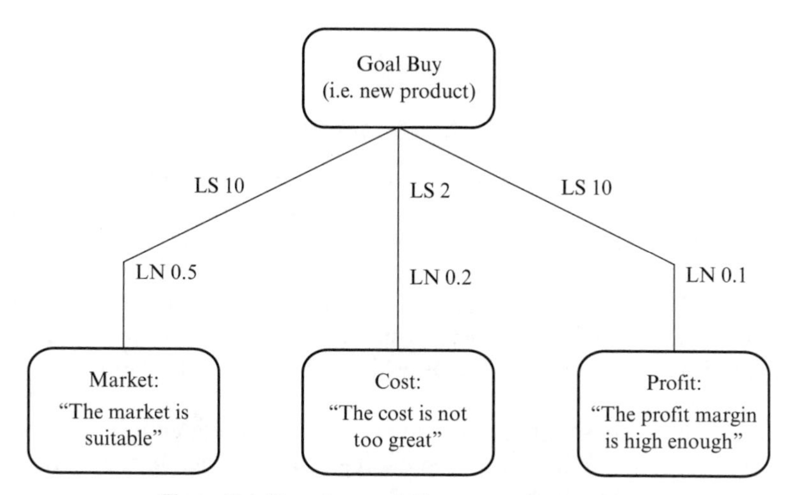


**Figure 7.1** Bayesian model for assessment system

Next a pair of weighting factors have to be assigned to each antecedent. These are the values of logical sufficiency (LS) and logical necessity (LN). The LS is the factor by which the odds of the goal's being true are multiplied, if the antecedent is true. The LN is the factor by which the odds of the goal's being true are multiplied, if the antecedent is false.

In the case of this example the meaning of "true" for each antecedent would be:

Market: "The market is suitable"
Cost: "The total cost is not too great"
Profit: "The profit margin is high enough"

To show the Bayesian dependency of Buy on Market, values of LS and LN have to be found and specified. Suppose in this case that:

Market LS10 LN0.5

This means that the likelihood of Buy's being true would be increased by a factor of 10, if Market were true (i.e. if the market were suitably large), but decreased by a factor of 0.5 if Market were false (i.e. if the market were too small). Again, other Bayesian dependencies would be specified in a similar way. Thus:

Cost LS2 LN0.2

would represent the view that it would be twice as likely for Buy to be true if Cost were true, but one-fifth as likely if Cost were false.

Suppose also that the values of LS and LN for the Profit were found to be:

Profit LS10 LN0.1

### *Answering questions with certainty factors*

In this example, there are three questions to be answered by the user. These are: Market, Cost and Profit. Sometimes, the user may not be certain of an answer and might want to express a level of confidence to reflect his or her uncertainty. For example, during a system run, the user may feel only 80% certain that the profit is large enough. The user can enter this value by setting the bar value when the question is answered (see Fig. 7.2). This is an unscaled bar for input and is called a certainty factor, which will be studied in more detail later in the chapter.

The certainty factor entered on the bar scale is translated into a number in the range 0.0 to +1.0 indicating the degree of confidence in the truth of the question on the following scale:

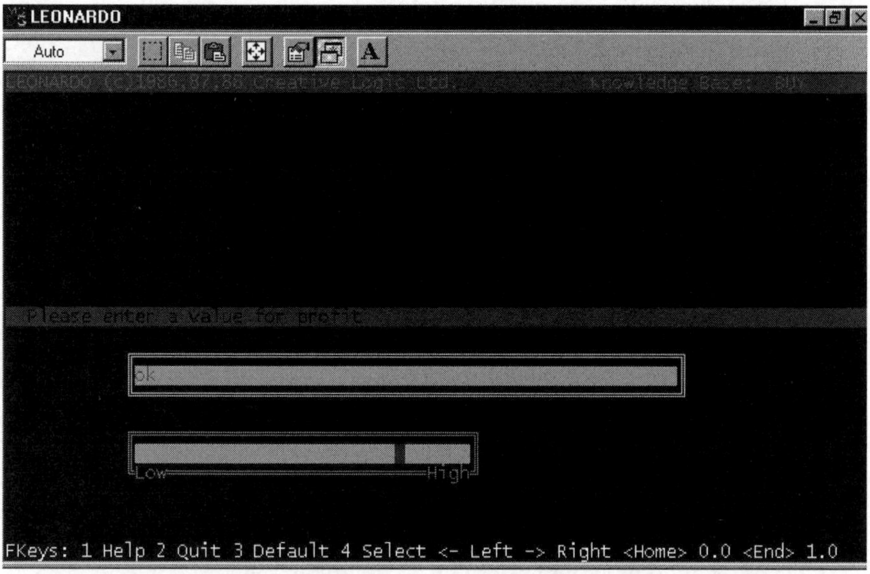

**Figure 7.2** Illustration of entering a CF with a question using the certainty bar

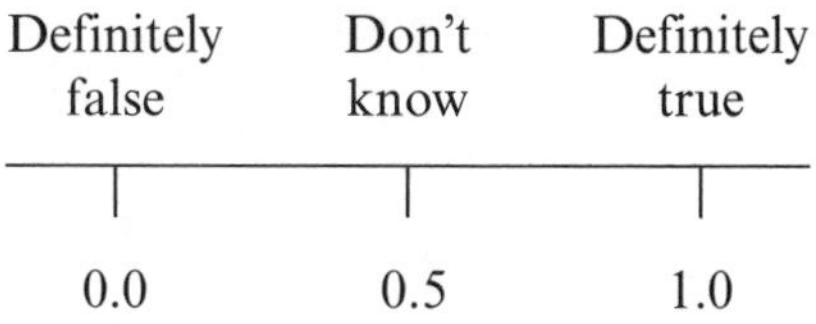

| Definitely false | Don't know | Definitely true |
|---|---|---|
| 0.0 | 0.5 | 1.0 |

In the definition of the Bayesian hypothesis given, it was assumed that the antecedent hypotheses were either true or false, corresponding to certainty factors of 0 and 1 respectively. If the certainty factor is intermediate, then the scaling factor used to update the probability of the goal hypothesis will be on a pro rata basis as given by the function shown in Fig. 7.3.

This means that if the certainty factor is 0.5 the odds of the goal's being true will be multiplied by 1, and so will remain the same. For instance, if in answer to the question "Is it true that a large market exists?" the reply given is between high and low or "don't know", then the a priori odds of Buy's being true will be multiplied by 1. In other words, not knowing whether a large market exists leaves the certainty of the goal Buy unchanged, as would be expected.

On the other hand, if a value of high is entered, then as the graph shows the a priori odds of Buy's being true will be multiplied by LS: that is, the logical sufficiency as expected. Finally, if a value of low is entered, then the a priori odds of Buy's being true will be multiplied by LS. The complete Leonardo listing is shown in Fig. 7.4.

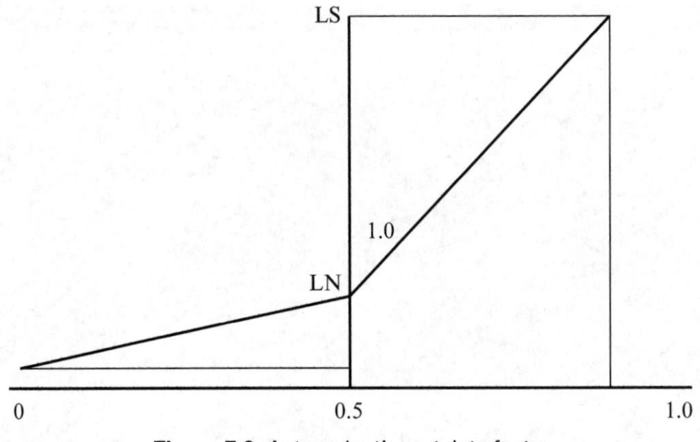


**Figure 7.3** Antecedent's certainty factor

```
_MainRuleSet_

/* CD retailer adviser system using Bayesian inference with Leonardo

control cf

control 'threshold 0.02'

ask profit

ask Market

ask cost

seek Buy

control bayes

   if Market is yes{LS 10 LN     0.5}
   then Buy is ok{prior        0.2}

   if cost is low {LS 2 LN 0.2}
   then Buy is ok

   if profit is good {LS 10 LN 0.1}
   then Buy is ok
```

**Figure 7.4** The complete Leonardo source code

### *Annotation of the Leonardo source code*

The goal of the system is to determine whether a particular item should be bought for stock. For brevity the goal is referred to as Buy. Without any prior knowledge the probability of this being true is 1 in 5.

The certainty of the Buy hypothesis depends on three factors: the existence of a large market, a reasonably small total outlay, and a good profit margin.

Quantitatively this dependency is as follows from the given values of LS and LN:

> If a large market exists, Buy becomes ten times more likely, but if not it becomes two times less likely.
>
> If the cost is OK, Buy becomes twice as likely, but if the outlay is too high Buy becomes 5 times less likely.
>
> If the profit is ok, Buy becomes 10 times more likely, but if it is too low then Buy becomes 10 times less likely.

A sample output screen is shown in Fig.7.5. The value given in parenthesis is the Bayesian probability calculated through the consultation.

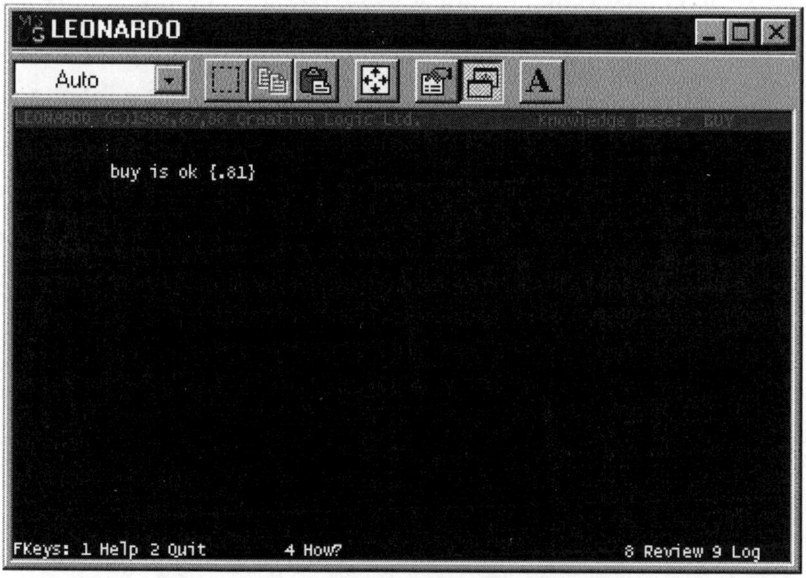

**Figure 7.5** Leonardo sample output for Buy product

## 7.4 Certainty factors

The well-known medical expert system MYCIN does not use Bayesian uncertainty for the following reasons:

- The difficulty in collecting prior and conditional probabilities. Difficulties arise from the amount of work involved in collecting these values from an expert.
- Possibility of non-disjointness of hypothesis. Bayes's theorem is valid only if the hypotheses are disjoint, meaning that there is no overlap. In the case of MYCIN, hypotheses are likely to be non-disjoint since one infectious disease, such as bronchitis, is likely to have a bearing on a patient having another, such as influenza.
- Incompleteness of hypothesis. One of the requirements for applying Bayes' theorem is that all possible hypotheses in a solution space must be considered. However, in a medical domain like MYCIN this may not happen because all possible diseases may not be known in advance. For example, AIDS was only discovered in the 1980s.
- Excessive calculations. MYCIN contains many hypotheses, so during a consultation many calculations would be necessary if a Bayesian model were used.

MYCIN has evolved using another numerical technique called *certainty factors.* Certainty factors are not probabilities because they are not necessarily measured on the probability scale [0,1]. Instead, MYCIN uses a certainty factor (CF) scale of [–1,1]. This CF scale is shown in Fig. 7.6. Notice that a value of CF = –1 corresponds to absolute falsehood. Conversely, a CF value of +1 corresponds to absolute certainty and a CF value of 0 corresponds to don't know. Recall that the expert system shell Leonardo used a CF scale of [0,1].

MYCIN uses some simple rules to manipulate CFs. They are:

- The CF of a disjunction of two hypotheses is calculated by taking the maximum CF of both. Put another way, this says that the measure of belief in the disjunction of the hypotheses is as strong as the belief in the one most strongly confirmed.
- The CF of a conjunction is found by taking the minimum of the CFs of the component conditions. The rationale here stems from an analogy with a chain that is only as strong as its weakest link.

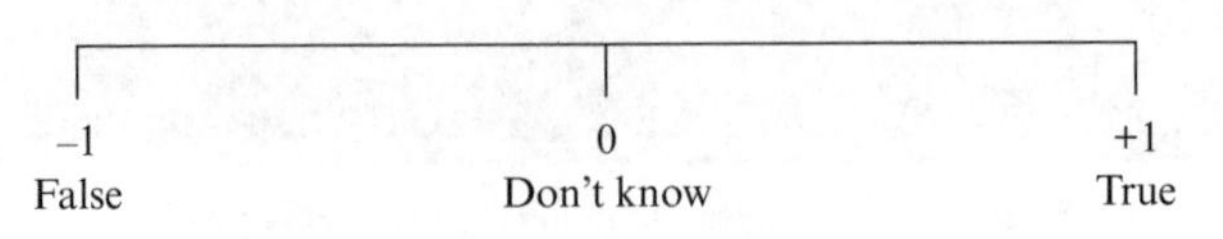


**Figure 7.6** Certainty factor scale for MYCIN

- When a rule fires and draws a conclusion, the data added to working memory by the action is assigned a CF equal to the product of the calculated CF of the premise and the CF associated with the action itself. For example, if there is a 50% CF that a piece of evidence leads to a conclusion, and only a 50% CF associated with the evidence itself, then there is only a 25% certainty factor associated with the final conclusion.

MYCIN has a measure of belief and a measure of disbelief associated with CFs, defined as follows:

$$\begin{aligned} \mathrm{MB}[H, E] &= \max[P(H/E), P(H)] - P(H) && \text{if } P(H) <> 1 \\ &= 1 && \text{if } P(H) = 1 \end{aligned}$$

$$\begin{aligned} \mathrm{MD}[H, E] &= \min[P(H/E), P(H)] - P(H) && \text{if } P(H) <> 0 \\ &= 1 && \text{if } P(H) = 0 \end{aligned}$$

A particular piece of evidence can either increase the probability of $H$, in which case $\mathrm{MB}[H, E] > 0$ and $\mathrm{MD}[H, E] = 0$ (i.e. there is no reason to disbelieve $H$), or decrease the probability of $H$, in which case $\mathrm{MD}[H, E] > 0$ and $\mathrm{MB}[H, E] = 0$.

From these two measures, the CF is:

$$\mathrm{CF}[H, E] = \mathrm{MB}[H,E] - \mathrm{MD}[H, E]$$

Note that if $\mathrm{CF} > 0$, this lends weight to the belief that the hypothesis is true. On the other hand, if $\mathrm{CF} < 0$, this provides more evidence against its truth.

## 7.5 Non-numerical methods for handling uncertainty

A useful way of classifying the techniques for inference under uncertainty is to divide them into those doing inference with uncertainty, and those doing inference about uncertainty. The former are those that include some numeric measure, namely probability. Some of these techniques have been considered in the previous section. The latter techniques have to maintain information about the source of the uncertainty. Examples of such an approach are non-monotonic logic and Cohen's theory of endorsement. These methods of uncertainty are not mutually exclusive and may be used together in some systems.

### *Non-monotonic logic*

In inference systems employing non-monotonic logic, assumptions are made that may have to be revised in the light of new information. They have the property that at any given stage more than one mutually consistent set of conclusions can be derived from the available data and possible assumptions. However, practical systems such as Doyle's Truth Maintenance System (TMS) produce only one such set at any stage. Such conclusions that are reached may be invalidated as new data may be incompatible with some of the default assumptions made. The inference system requires that the justifications for any conclusions are recorded during the inference process and used for dependency-directed backtracking during the revision of beliefs. Non-monotonic logic is particularly useful for reasoning under incomplete information. The reasoning process calls for the use of as many assumptions as possible without producing a logical inconsistency. For more on TMS see Rich (1992).

### *Theory of endorsements*

Cohen and Grindberg (1993) describe a theory of reasoning about uncertainty based on a representation of states of certainty called *endorsements*. The theory is a departure from numerical methods of reasoning. Instead of propagating numbers, knowledge about the uncertainty itself is propagated. This knowledge includes strength of evidence, whether the evidence is for or against, provability, etc. Instead of combining all uncertainties into a number, the theory allows domain-dependent heuristics to do the ranking and discounting of uncertainty.

## 7.6 Summary

A range of methods for handling uncertainty in expert systems have been discussed in this chapter. Table 7.3 summarises the main numeric and non-numeric techniques.

---

## Exercises

1. The prior probability that a patient at a hospital has meningitis is 0.02. The probability that a patient who has a fever given that the patient has meningitis is 0.85, and the probability that a patient has a fever given that the patient does not have meningitis is 0.05. Find the probability that a patient with a fever has meningitis.
2. What are the knowledge acquisition difficulties associated with the use of Bayes' theorem for handling uncertainty? Choose a diagnostic domain to illustrate your answer.
3. What are the problems with obtaining subjective probability values from a domain expert? How would these difficulties be resolved in practice?

Table 7.3 *Comparison summary of uncertainty techniques*

| *Technique* | *Motivation* | *Advantages* | *Disadvantages* |
|---|---|---|---|
| Bayesian | Quantification of uncertainty characterised by subjective weights | Precise, based on mathematical probability | Complex mathematics makes it difficult to implement in practice systems |
| Certainty factors | Quantification of uncertainty relating to heuristic knowledge represented as rules | Distinguishes between supporting and detracting evidence | *Ad hoc*, not based upon precise mathematics |
| Non-numeric methods | Emphasis on reasoning about uncertainty rather than with uncertainty | Precise | Highly representation dependent, difficult to implement in practical systems |

**4.** Discuss the reasons why certainty factors are such a popular form of representing uncertainty in rule-based systems. Use examples to illustrate your answers.

**5.** Some approaches to implementing uncertainty in an expert system depend on one's belief. Justify why a user should trust an expert system whose knowledge is based on the beliefs of an expert.

**6.** Access the Web site of Bayes Corp. (http://www.bayes.com).
   (a) Identify their products.
   (b) Identify two projects that have applied Bayesian uncertainty.

## References and further reading

Cohen, P. and Grindberg, M. (1983) A framework for heuristic reasoning about uncertainty. *IJCAI Proceedings*.

Duda, R., Hart, K., Konolige, K. and Reboh, R. (1979) *A Computer Based Consultant for Mineral Exploration*, SRI International, Technical Report.

Giarratano, J. C. and Riley, G. D. (1992) *Expert Systems: Principles and Programming*, Boston: PWS Kent.

Rich, E. (1992) *Artificial Intelligence*, 2nd edition, New York: McGraw-Hill.

Shortliffe, E. H. (1976) *Computer Based Medical Consultations*, New York: Elsevier.

CHAPTER 8

# *Human–computer interaction issues for expert systems*

**Objectives**

In this chapter you will learn:

- to appreciate user interface requirements for expert systems;
- to distinguish between the knowledge engineer's interface and the user interface;
- to be aware of the interface styles appropriate for expert systems;
- to be aware of the requirements of explanation facilities for expert systems;
- to know what methods are available to improve explanation facilities in rule-based systems.

## 8.1 Introduction

Human–computer interation (HCI) is as important an issue in the design of an expert system as it is with a conventional system. Indeed, it could be argued that it is more important because of the highly interactive nature of such systems. Oakley (1980) has argued that output from conventional systems based on the certainties of mathematics and Boolean algebra cannot be questioned, but for an expert system the output is at best a probability, which may or may not be correct. This means that it is essential that the user can interrogate the system and query the output, asking questions to establish the key rules that determine the answer, as well as asking questions to establish how firm the answer is when parameters are changed.

There is a broad consensus of agreement that successful expert systems in the future will rely heavily on advances in HCI. Amongst the advances will be the need to provide more conceptual guidance to users and builders of expert systems, as well as better-quality explanation and improved input/output architectures. This chapter examines the design issues for improving the quality of human interaction in expert systems.

## 8.2 Requirements for expert systems interfaces

Many of the HCI design issues for expert systems are the same as those for a conventional system. The nature of interaction in an expert system, however, is such that the interfaces for expert systems may have additional needs, for expert systems create a different set of demands on the interface (Hendler and Lewis 1992). Unlike a conventional program, an expert system is not just a tool that implements a process, but rather a representation of that process. Furthermore, many of these processes have implications in that the judgements made by such systems have critical real-world consequences – judgements that often involve reasoning under uncertainty. The user interface must present not only conclusions, but also an explication of how those conclusions were reached. A number of interface styles for both the knowledge engineer and the end-user are in widespread use. Some of these are briefly discussed in the next section.

## 8.3 Knowledge engineer's interface and user interface

There is a clear distinction between the knowledge engineer's interface and the end-user interface. The former provides access to the tools for building the expert system, such as an editor, testing and debugging facilities, explanation facilities to enable the knowledge engineer to check the program correctness, and so on. The latter provides access to the operation of the expert system, enabling an end-user to consult the system, with access to questions being asked and advice given, as well as explanation facilities, possibly on-line help support, and so on. Clearly, the expert may also need access to the knowledge engineer's interface during the development of the expert system to confirm the correctness of the program operation. Moreover, the end-user will also need to "test the expert system" for acceptability. The relationship between the various personnel, that is the expert, the end-user and the knowledge engineer, and the expert system is shown in Fig. 8.1.

## 8.4 Input and output devices for expert systems

There are many input and output devices that are available for communication between the user and the expert system. The most common input devices are: mouse, keyboard, light pen, touch-sensitive screen, and voice input. Typical output devices include monitor, printer, graph plotters, and so on. An expert system interaction will normally take the form of a set of questions, using one or more such input devices, usually followed by some advice from the system using one or more output devices. This advice from the expert system might take the form of textual or graphical output depending on the nature of the

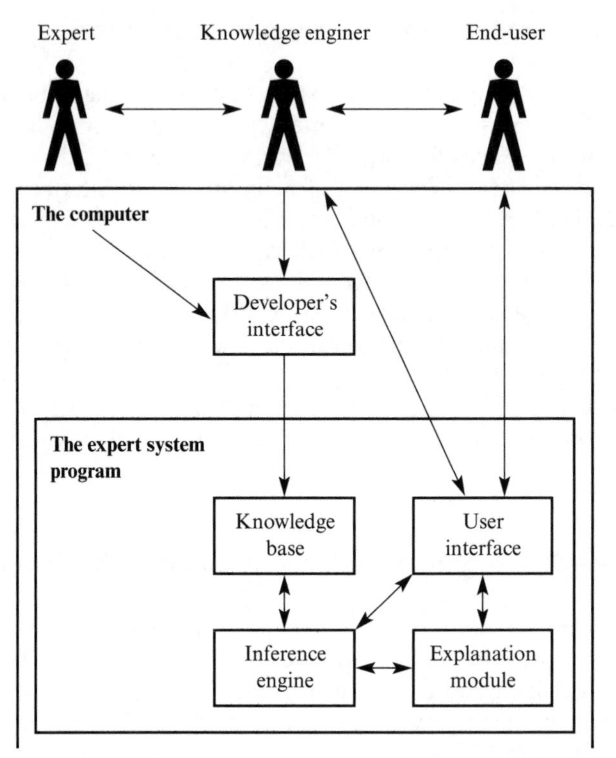


**Figure 8.1** Relationship between expert system personnel

expert system domain. For example, it may be more appropriate to display the advice from a machine fault expert system in graphical form, so that the user would find it easier to locate the fault. On the other hand, textual output may be more appropriate for output in a legal expert system.

---

## Self-assessment exercise

Why is the keyboard the most common form of input device for the majority of expert systems that have been developed to date?

---

## 8.5 Human interaction styles appropriate for expert systems

Several interface styles are available for developers and users of expert systems. Many of these styles have been borrowed from conventional software systems. The most common in use are the following.

Welcome to the housing benefit expert system

1. What is your name?
   *Fred Flintstone*
2. Are you currently employed?
   *No*
3. How much money do you have saved?
   *£7,500*

**Figure 8.2** Sample of questions taken from housing benefit expert system

### *Direct keyboard entry*

Direct keyboard entry in which a user responds to a question by typing the answer with a keyboard is the oldest form of interaction style. An example of this type of interaction is shown in Fig. 8.2. This example is taken from a local authority housing benefit expert system. (Note: computer questions are shown in normal type, user replies are shown in italics.)

### *Menu interface styles*

If the questions in Fig. 8.2 are examined carefully, then direct keyboard entry is the only viable option for questions 1 and 3 because enumerating all possible choices for these questions would be impractical. However, question 2 would be better suited to a menu interface style. A menu interface style allows the user to select from a list of options that are visible on the screen. The user may then select the appropriate choice by highlighting using the keyboard or, perhaps, the mouse. For example, a menu interface style may be more appropriate for question 2 as shown in Fig. 8.3.

A menu interface style is often preferable to direct keyboard entry because it saves time in typing and reduces typing errors, since the user is forced to make selections only from a menu list of choices that are available.

Question 2. Are you currently employed? (Please select yes or no)
Yes
No

**Figure 8.3** A menu question

### *Some guidelines for menu interface design*

- Try to group logically related options together either as menu block options or in separate menu screens.
- Try to order menu options by operational sequence, frequency of use and importance of use.
- Indicate the reply expected where possible and associate it with the option.
- Title the menu according to its function.
- Give the user feedback about menu levels, errors and so on.
- Provide escape routes and bypasses if possible.
- Bullet-proof the replies. For example, if 1 to 7 are options and 0 is escape, make sure that any other keystroke is followed by an error message and not a program failure.

### *Natural language*

A natural language interface is a communication style in which the user enters commands in a well-defined subset of some natural language such as English.

### *Forms*

These are interface styles that enable a user to enter data by typing, or otherwise, into predetermined positions that would be displayed on the screen.

### *Iconic*

In the iconic interface user commands and system feedback are expressed in graphical symbols or pictograms instead of words. This type of interface style is very common in the Windows 98 environment.

### *Direct manipulation*

Direct manipulation refers to an interface style in which the user manipulates, through a language of button pushes and movements of a pointing device such as a mouse, a graphic representation of the underlying data.

### *User acceptance issues*

A successful expert system will depend upon how comfortable the user feels with the system. It is essential, therefore, to involve users at a very early stage in the development of the interface to an expert system. The key issues regarding the user interface design are:

- Interface design should be user centred. This means that an interface should interact with users on their terms, should be logical and consistent, and should include facilities to help users with the system and to recover from their mistakes.
- Designing an interface metaphor is often a good way to help users with a system. *Webster's Dictionary* defines metaphor as "a figure of speech in which a word or phrase denoting one kind of action is used in place of another to suggest a likeness or analogy between them". Metaphors aid users in understanding a new target domain (e.g. a word processor) by allowing them to comprehend it (up to the point of "mismatch" ) in terms of a source domain (e.g. a typewriter). Metaphors aid designers because adoption of a metaphor allows them to structure aspects of the target system interface in terms of familiar and commonly understood aspects of the source domain (Erickson 1995).
- Selecting an appropriate interface style. WIMP interfaces may be appropriate if the user has access to a graphical user interface such as Windows 98. Menu systems are good for casual users because they have a low learning overhead; they can be tedious to use when the number of options is very large. Command language interfaces may be popular with regular, experienced users because complex commands can be created and they can be faster than menu systems. Graphical information display should be used when it is intended to present information in the form of trends and approximate values. Digital display should be used only when precision is required.
- On-line help is no longer regarded as a luxury for conventional software users but a necessity. The same is true for expert system users. These users should get support on how to perform various tasks, such as changing an answer to a question, as well as support with information about the application domain.
- Appropriate design should be included for handling errors. Error messages should never be accusatory and suggest that the user is to blame. They should offer suggestions about how to repair the error and provide a link to a help system.
- Colour must be used very carefully to prevent confusing the user. The colour combinations should be consistent and appropriate. For example, if the background colour used for error message windows is red, then this colour should be used consistently throughout the application design.

### *Icon design principles*

The following issues should be considered when designing an icon-based interface:

- Test the representation of the icons with users.
- Wherever possible use metaphors from the user's domain.
- Make icons as realistic as possible.
- Give the icon a clear outline to help visual discrimination.
- Avoid symbols unless their meaning is already known.
- When showing commands use a concrete representation.

## 8.6 Explanation facilities

In Chapter 2, it was seen that expert systems are capable of explaining their reasoning processes. Explanation facilities have had much value in convincing sceptical users of expert systems of the validity of their advice. Some researchers believed that explanation facilities could do even more by teaching novice users a better understanding of the application domain. An attempt to turn the highly influential medical expert system MYCIN into a teaching program for students was made for this very purpose and failed. This section will examine the reasons for this and discuss ways in which explanation facilities can be improved.

### *The need for explanation facilities*

The ability to explain their reasoning processes has been seen as a key feature of expert systems. Explanation facilities provide the user with a means of understanding the behaviour of the expert system. Research has shown (Wolverton 1995) that users of expert systems make good use of explanation facilities. This is clearly important because a consultation with a human expert will often require some explanation. Many people would not always accept the answers of an expert without some form of justification. For example, an obese patient who has been advised to undertake a special diet may ask for an explanation concerning why it is being recommended so that the patient is aware of any risks, alternatives, likelihood of success, and so on.

### *Rule trace explanations*

The built-in explanation facilities on most existing expert systems are generally agreed to be inadequate (Morris 1987, Rogers 1989). The explanation given by an expert system may not provide answers to the range of questions that would be available from a human expert. This is because the scope of the knowledge available by many rule-based expert systems is often limited to problem-solving explanations. This means that such an explanation is limited to how the system arrived at the advice given without giving any justification. To gain a better

| | |
|---|---|
| RULE 1 | *if* temperature <55<br>then room is cool |
| RULE 2 | *if* temperature >=55<br>and temperature <65<br>then room is warm |
| RULE 3 | *if* temperature >=65<br>then room is hot |
| RULE 4 | *if* light is poor<br>and room is cool<br>then best plant is ivy |
| RULE 5 | *if* light is poor<br>and room is hot<br>then best plant is cheese plant |
| RULE 6 | *if* light is bright<br>and room is warm<br>then best plant is asparagus fern |
| RULE 7 | *if* light is bright<br>and room is hot<br>then best plant is begonia rex |
| QUESTION | light is bright, poor, good |
| QUESTION | temperature |

**Figure 8.4** House plant knowledge base

understanding of the knowledge required for a good explanation, consider the extract of rules taken from a house plant advisor expert system as shown in Fig. 8.4. Consider what happens when this knowledge base is combined with a simple backward-chaining inference engine.

Given that the expert system is trying to find the best house plant using backward chaining, it will search for the first rule in the knowledge base with house plant in the conclusion. This is RULE 4, "best plant is ivy". To prove this conclusion in RULE 4, it is necessary to prove that the values for the two conditions in this rule are true. That is, "room is cool" and "light is poor". The condition "light is poor" would be found by asking the user for its value since it is not a rule conclusion: "light is poor" is a question to the user. However, the "room is cool" condition is found by trying to prove RULE 1 because it is a conclusion of this rule. This means that the conditions for RULE 1, namely "temperature <55", must be true for this condition to be true. The value for this condition would be found by asking the user to input the temperature value. If the user were to input a value for the temperature >55, then RULE 1 would clearly fail, since the condition "temperature <55" has failed. Consequently, RULE 4 would also fail, since the condition "room is cool" has also failed. In this event, the inference engine would seek the next rule in the knowledge base with best house plant in the conclusion. This is RULE 5, with "best plant is cheese plant", and proceed in the same way as it did in trying to prove RULE 4.

### *The rule trace*

The above inference-chaining process is completely transparent because the problem-solving knowledge, that is the rules, are written explicitly. Thus, an explanation is available to the user that can provide a "rule trace" of the expert system's execution during a consultation. Such an explanation facility is therefore called a rule trace. This means that the user can obtain *problem-solving* explanations detailing which rules were invoked to reach a conclusion. For example, if, given the above expert system, the conclusion of the best house plant was ivy, then the user could find out "how" the expert system arrived at that conclusion. The resulting response from the expert system might be something like:

> In RULE 1, I found room is cool
> Because RULE 1, condition temperature <55 is true (user input value).
>
> In RULE 4, I also found light is poor from direct user input
> THEREFORE conclusion of RULE 4 is true, i.e. best plant is ivy.

The rule trace can provide two basic explanation queries: *how* and *why*. A how query enables a user to find out how the expert system arrived at a conclusion; see the example above. A why query enables a user to find out why a particular question is being asked. For example, consider the following dialogue between a user and the house plant expert system:

*Expert system:* What is the temperature of the room in degrees Fahrenheit?
*User:* Why?
*Expert system:* I am trying to prove RULE 4, the best plant is ivy. To do this I need to prove RULE 1, room is cool. To do this I need to find the temperature of the room in degrees Fahrenheit from the user.
*Expert system:* What is the temperature of the room in degrees Fahrenheit?
*User:* 38.
*Expert system:* What is the quality of light in the room: bright, poor, good?
*User:* Why?
*Expert system:* I am trying to prove RULE 4, best plant is ivy. To do this I need to find the quality of light of the room from the user.
*Expert system:* What is the quality of light in the room: bright, poor, good?
*User:* Poor.
*Expert system:* The best plant is ivy.

### *Problems with rule traces*

Rule traces providing *how* and *why* queries form the foundation of nearly all explanation facilities to date. The main drawback with rule traces is that the explanation merely links problem and solution; it presents the chain of reasoning constructed by the system. This means that the system knows how a conclusion is reached but it does not know why that knowledge is there in the first place. For example, if the expert system contains a rule of the form above "IF room is cool and light is poor, THEN best plant is ivy", then it cannot explain by justifying the truth of this rule, but merely execute the conclusion if the conditions become true. To justify this rule it would need access to the deeper theoretical knowledge of an expert. In other words, a rule trace can reconstruct its problem-solving behaviour by using its knowledge base, but it cannot justify the existence of that knowledge base itself. This is because the deeper theoretical knowledge is not explicitly available. Of course, this does not matter if the expert system is to be used for problem-solving only. However, this lack of justification knowledge becomes an impediment if expert systems are to be used as learning tools. Clancey (1983) realised this when he attempted to use the medical expert system MYCIN to teach students how to go about identifying organisms, because the resulting program GUIDON was not very successful. The reason was that on examining MYCIN, it was discovered that important knowledge lay hidden in the structure of the rules. In order to provide a satisfactory explanation of what was going on, GUIDON needed to have this knowledge explicitly available. Providing a deeper model of the domain is one possible solution.

### *Shallow and deep knowledge*

The inability to provide justification knowledge occurs because the model of the domain does not capture all the forms of knowledge used by experts in their reasoning. This is called *deep knowledge*, and experts would have access to such knowledge, although when an expert tackles a problem, he or she will often draw upon heuristic knowledge or "rules of thumb". This is called *shallow knowledge*, and experts use easily memorised shallow knowledge as an aid to solve problems rapidly. For example, a paramedic nurse might check on the pupil of a patient's eye to find out if the patient has taken a barbiturate drug overdose. This is shallow simplified knowledge derived from a deeper causal model of human physiology knowledge. It is this shallow knowledge that is usually captured in expert system form because it is clearly much easier to obtain and frequently sufficient for problem solving. However, a deep representation will normally improve the explanation facilities.

### *The XPLAIN system*

Swartout (1986) also realised that rule-based systems were unable to justify what they were doing because the knowledge to produce justifications was not in the system. His XPLAIN system was one of the first to concentrate on explanation using automatic programming techniques to record the design rationale behind the construction of expert system explanation. However, this process is difficult to implement in practical systems.

### *Strategic knowledge*

Consider again the house plant knowledge base in Fig. 8.1. It was seen that if RULE 4 were to fail, then the inference engine would try to prove the next rule in the sequence in which they are written with best house plant in the conclusion, that is RULE 5. Note that the order in which the inference engine is trying to find the best plant is implicit in the ordering of the rules. Thus, the knowledge describing the order in which the solution is sought is not visible. Clancey (1983) also realised this when he discovered that GUIDON was unable to explain its system strategies; as in the house plant system he realised that the search strategy was implicit in the rules and thus the knowledge was not available for inspection.

As Clancey says:

> In attempting to 'transfer back' the expert's knowledge through GUIDON, we find that the expert's diagnostic approach and understanding of rules have not been explicitly represented. GUIDON cannot justify the rules because MYCIN does not have an encoding of how the concepts in a rule fit

> together. GUIDON cannot fully articulate MYCIN's problem solving approach because the structure of the search space and the strategy for traversing it are implicit in the ordering of the rule concepts. Thus, the seemingly straightforward task of converting a knowledge based system into a computer aided instruction program has led to a detailed re-examination of the rule base and the foundations upon which rules are constructed.

Clancey's follow-up system, called NEOMYCIN (Clancey 1983), extended MYCIN's capability to include strategic explanations. *Strategic knowledge* is knowledge about how to approach a problem by choosing an ordering on methods and rules that minimises efforts in the search for a solution. Table 8.1 summarises the different types of knowledge required for explanation. In NEOMYCIN the strategic knowledge takes the form of meta-rules, which are grouped into abstract tasks quite independent of the knowledge domain. These meta-rules can be thought of as "floating above" the domain knowledge base.

### Canned text

Canned text has been used in some systems with moderate success for some time now. As its name suggests, canned text uses previously prepared text to enhance explanations. A quintessential use of canned text is in the develop-

Table 8.1 *Knowledge required for explanations*

| *Knowledge required* | *Purpose and effect upon explanation* | *Possible method of implementation in rule-based expert systems* |
|---|---|---|
| Problem solving | Presenting the chain of reasoning constructed by the system by providing a trace of the problem-solving path. The effect will link the problem with the solution | Always available, without any additional effort |
| Justification | To justify the existence of knowledge in the expert system. The effect will be to give users more confidence in the correctness of the knowledge base | Can be included if required by including a "deep model" of the domain |
| Strategic | To show how one line of reasoning was constructed rather than another. The effect will be to give users an insight into the methods used for minimising the search for a solution | Can be implemented by using meta-rules explicitly outlining solution strategy |

ment of computer error messages. By anticipating all the questions that users are likely to ask the system builder can map system responses to a detailed "English-like" explanation which the user would find more acceptable than a simple rule trace. However, the system builder has to anticipate all the possible user questions in advance in order to invoke the appropriate response. Canned text, unlike rule traces, is also very domain dependent, making it very difficult to reuse in other systems. Also, as Sparck-Jones (1984) argues, the provision of canned text can mislead the user into overestimating the system's capabilities, because users may believe they are communicating in natural language with the system.

## 8.7 Uses of hypermedia

In recent years, much energy has been devoted to the synthesis of expert system and hypermedia in an attempt to build systems more acceptable to the user (Bielawski and Lewand 1991). Hypermedia is a means of linking text, graphics or sound by using a pointing mechanism. Hypertext is specifically concerned with linking only text. This has become a well-known medium for linking World Wide Web pages on the Internet. Hypermedia is a management information tool that links graphics, sound, text, etc., in an associative way. In doing so, it allows a user to navigate through a system in a non-linear manner. Internet software browsers such as Netscape Navigator and Microsoft's Internet Explorer make use of hypertext by allowing users to click on words or graphic images that will link the word to more information. Hypertext has been used successfully in many expert systems. Figure 8.5 shows a fragment from a statistical adviser expert system that uses hypertext links to add explanation to the description of statistical tests. The system has been written using the expert system shell for Windows called KnowledgePro. In the top window of Fig. 8.5, the phrase Kendalls Coefficient of Concordance is underlined. This means that it is a hypertext word, which the user can click with the mouse to get additional explanation. The bottom screen of Fig. 8.5 shows the text in the pop-up window that accompanies this explanation. Notice that the phrase Kendalls Coefficient of Concordance appears in the title bar of the lower window. Hypertext allows users with differing degrees of expertise to use the system on terms that may be appropriate to their level.

## 8.8 Graphical interfaces

There have been a number of expert systems developed that already have some form of graphical interface. Many of these, however, have been highly application-specific representations, which could not be generalised to other domains.

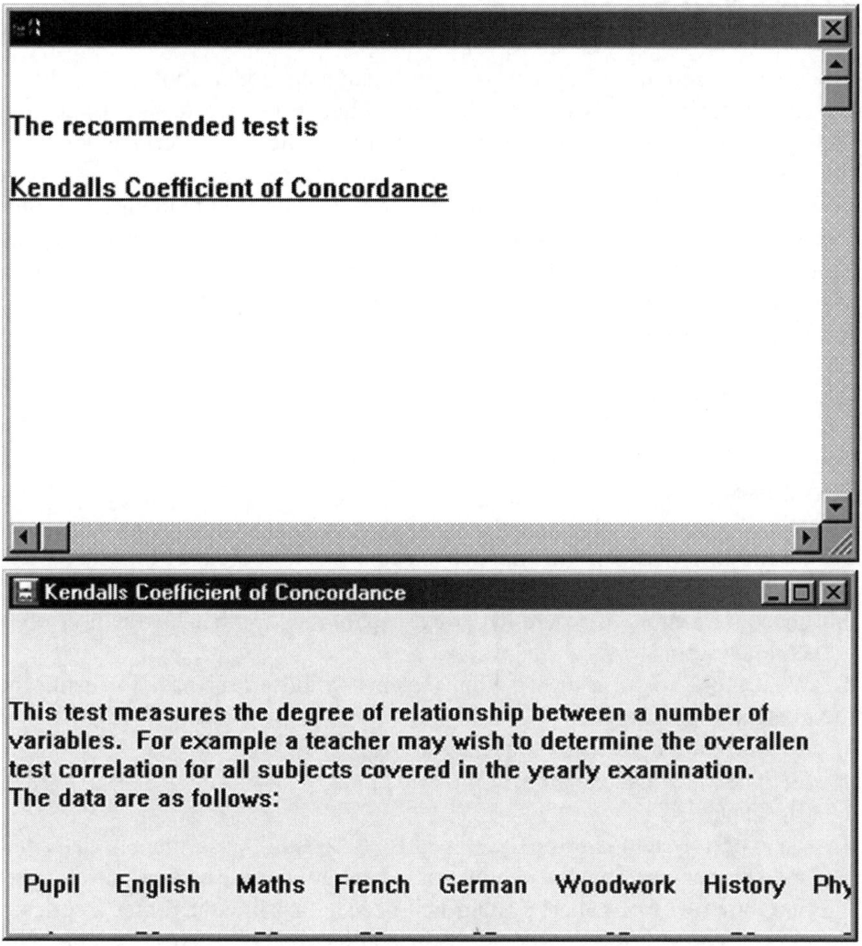

The recommended test is

Kendalls Coefficient of Concordance

Kendalls Coefficient of Concordance

This test measures the degree of relationship between a number of variables. For example a teacher may wish to determine the overallen test correlation for all subjects covered in the yearly examination.
The data are as follows:

Pupil English Maths French German Woodwork History Phy

**Figure 8.5** Example of hypertext links in KnowledgePro for Windows

STEAMER (Hollan, Hutchins and Weitzman 1984) is probably the most cited of all graphically based systems and is an interactive, simulation-based training system for steam propulsion in the US Navy domain. A pre-existing detailed mathematical model of a steam propulsion system was used, and STEAMER added a graphical interface to that simulation. STEAMER provides multiple views of the system and allows manipulation of the system at different hierarchical levels. Views range from abstract high-level representations to more specific views of subsystems. However, STEAMER was not built with the conventional expert system goal of replacing a human expert. Instead, the goal was based on "discovery learning" by providing an interactive expert system environment that helps a person to understand a complex domain.

## 8.9 Conclusions

The success of an expert system is often highly dependent upon the quality of the user interface. This chapter has examined interface design issues and included guidelines for enhancing the quality of the user interface. However, the difficulties in designing user interfaces for expert systems do not seem to be in the area of building commercial-grade interfaces but in matching the interface to the user's cognitive task. (Stelzner and Williams 1992). This is because expert system users differ not only in their level of expertise but also in their requirements. A great deal is also made of the capability of explanation facilities in expert systems. However, as this chapter has also shown, such facilities are sometimes limited in scope, and without additional effort by the expert system builder may not be adequate.

---

## Exercises

1. Distinguish between the knowledge engineer's and the user interface. What facilities would you expect to find in a knowledge engineer's interface?
2. Give an example of where hypertext capabilities can benefit the user of an expert system.
3. What is the *why* question? What reasons would a user have for using this explanation facility?
4. What are the benefits of the rule trace to:
   (a) The knowledge engineer
   (b) The user?
5. An expert system is to be developed to assist bank customers in determining whether they may be eligible for a bank loan and the amount that they may borrow. The expert system will need to ask the customer a series of questions such as "Are you in full-time employment?", "How long have you resided at your current address?", and so on. Explain how the provision of hypertext may assist a user in this type of expert system.
6. The users of many expert systems often turn out to be "experts". For instance, several experienced medical consultants are known to use MYCIN, the medical expert system, on a regular basis. Why do you think an expert may benefit from using a system in which he or she has expert knowledge?

### *References and further reading*

Bielawski, L. and Lewand, R. (1991) *Intelligent System Design*, New York: John Wiley.

Chandrasekaran, B., Tanner, M. C. and Josephson, J. R. (1988) Explanation: the role of control strategies and deep models. In *Expert Systems: The User Interface*, Norwood, NJ: Ablex.

Clancey, W. J. (1983) Epistemology of a rule-based expert system: A framework for explanation. *AI Magazine*, vol. 20, no. 3, 215–251.

Erickson, T. D. (1995) Working with interface metaphors. From *Readings in HCI Towards the Year 2000*, San Francisco: Morgan Kaufman.
Hendler, J. and Lewis, C. (1992) Designing interfaces for expert systems. In *Expert Systems: The User Interface*, Norwood, NJ: Ablex.
Hollan, J. D. Hutchins, E. L. and Weitzman, L. (1984) STEAMER: an interactive inspectable simulation-based training system. *AI Magazine*, vol. 5, no. 2, 15–27.
Kidd, A. L. and Cooper, M. B. (1983) Man–machine interface for an expert system. *Proceedings of the BCS Group for Expert Systems*, Cambridge: Cambridge University Press.
Morris, A. (1987) Expert systems interface insight. *BCS Proceedings of HCI Conference*, Cambridge: Cambridge University Press.
Rogers, Y. (1989) What, when, how – explanation facilities. Open University Document, Dept. of Computing.
Southwick, R. (1986) Topic explanations in expert systems. *BCS Proceedings of the UK Expert Systems Conference*, Cambridge: Cambridge University Press.
Sparck-Jones, K. (1984) Natural language interfaces for expert systems. *BCS Proceedings of the UK Expert Systems Conference*. Cambridge: Cambridge University Press.
Swartout, W. (1986) Knowledge needed for expert systems explanation. *Future Computing Systems*, vol. 1, 91–144.
Stelzner, M. and Williams, M. D. (1992) The evaluation of interface requirements for expert systems. In *Expert Systems: The User Interface*, Norwood, NJ: Ablex.
Wolverton, M. (1995) Presenting significant information in expert system explanation. *Proceedings of the 7th AI Conference in Portugal*, Berlin: Springer.

CHAPTER 9

# *Introduction to design of expert systems using rule-based shells*

**Objectives**

In this chapter you will learn:

- to appreciate the stages in the design of an expert system;
- to prepare Mockler charts;
- to derive decision tables from Mockler charts;
- to write rule-sets from decision tables;
- to implement source code in a target expert system shell.

## 9.1 Introduction

The following section outlines the main stages involved in the design of an expert system using rules and implementation with the rule-based shell called VP-Expert. The example could well have been implemented in many of the other shells described in this book. A more detailed description of the commands of VP-Expert follows in the next chapter, and details of the VP-Expert environment are included in the Appendix.

## 9.2 Stages involved in the design of expert systems

The main stages for designing an expert system are:

1. Isolate an area of the domain for prototyping.
2. Target a decision to be prototyped.
3. Create a Mockler chart.
4. Create decision tables.
5. Encode using an appropriate shell.

### *Scenario*

A description of how the stages outlined above would be applied in practice is given in the following example. An expert system is to be built for use by benefit staff in a local authority to determine the recommendations for benefit payments. The system should provide advice for family credit, housing benefit, and single-parent benefits. Figure 9.1 shows a block diagram outlining the main tasks within the benefits system.

### *Isolate an area of the domain for prototyping*

Given the initial complexity of an expert system domain, it is often easier to begin by concentrating on a subsection of the domain for the development of a prototype. In the block diagram shown in Fig. 9.1, the area chosen to be isolated for developing the prototype is the emboldened "housing benefit" subsection.

### *Target a decision to be prototyped*

Having selected this subsection of the domain, the next step is to target a decision to be prototyped. A natural choice here is the recommended support level for a claimant. For example, the claimant may be eligible for a range of support levels, ranging from no support to total support. The block diagram given in Fig. 9.2 focuses on this subset of the domain and defines the critical factors involved in arriving at a decision.

The factors are:

- *House need.* Is the claimant in genuine need of accommodation? Two items influence the answer to this question: whether the claimant has a current fixed abode, and, if so, whether the fixed abode is adequate for the claimant's needs. Values for these two items will be obtained from questions to be answered by the user during run-time.

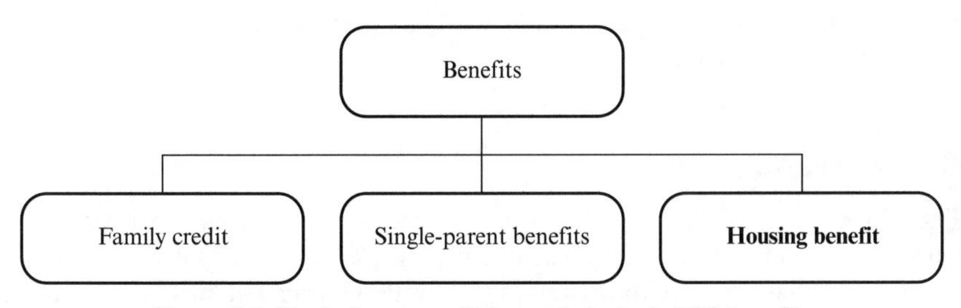


**Figure 9.1** Block diagram outlining main tasks in DSS benefits

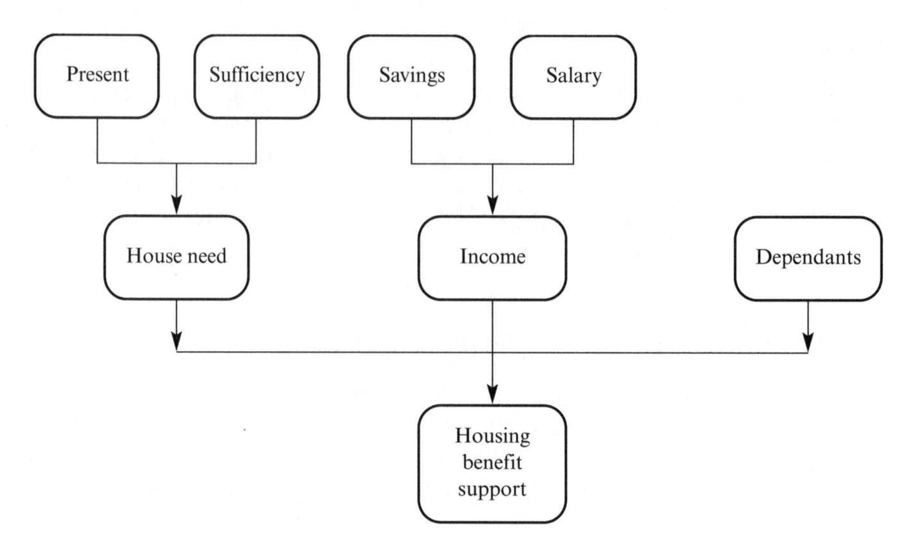


**Figure 9.2** Block diagram of decision to be prototyped

- *Income*. Does the claimant have insufficient income to live without housing benefit? Two items again influence the answer to this question: whether the claimant has any savings, and the salary of the claimant. Values for these two items will be obtained from questions to be answered by the user during run-time.
- *Dependants*. Does the claimant have any dependent relatives, children, etc.? The answer to this question is clearly a known fact and not dependent on any other factors. Therefore, this will be a question to be answered by the user during run-time.

Depending on the answers given, the client would be offered a service as follows:

- Level 1 support – applicants are awarded maximum benefit.
- Level 2 support – applicants are awarded a maximum of 80% support.
- Level 3 support – applicants are awarded a maximum of 50% support.
- Level 4 support – applicants are awarded a maximum of 20% support.
- No benefit whatsoever.

### *Mockler charts*

The block diagram in Fig. 9.2 is a useful way of describing the relationship between the factors and the goal, but it is not a diagram that lends itself to writing the rules for developing the expert system because it lacks the necessary detail. A type of diagram is required that shows the relationship between the factors that influence the goal along with input questions, rules, and recommendations made by the prototype. A *Mockler chart* or *dependency chart* (Mockler 1993) is a type of diagram suitable for this task.

To produce a Mockler chart, begin by turning the block diagram given in Fig. 9.2 horizontal. Next, draw boxes with triangles appended for any critical factors identified in step 2. In this application, the factors are house need, dependants and income. Because the dependants box feeds directly into recommendation, the intermediate box can be deleted from the Mockler chart. Then, on each straight line entering a triangle, write a word or phrase that best describes the item that will influence the outcome of the critical factor. This item is called a "variable". Under the straight line list all the possible values that the variable can take. Also write names for the values that the critical factor itself can have under each box that represents a critical factor. Do the same for the recommendation box. Figure 9.3 shows the completed Mockler chart.

### *The decision table*

The final step before generating the rules in the knowledge base is to create a *decision table*. The decision table is necessary to show the interrelationships of values to the outcome of any intermediate phase or final recommendation of the system. A separate decision table will be required for each dependent factor (i.e. triangle variable) in the Mockler chart. Thus, a decision table will need to be constructed for the factors of benefit, house need and income. Start by con-

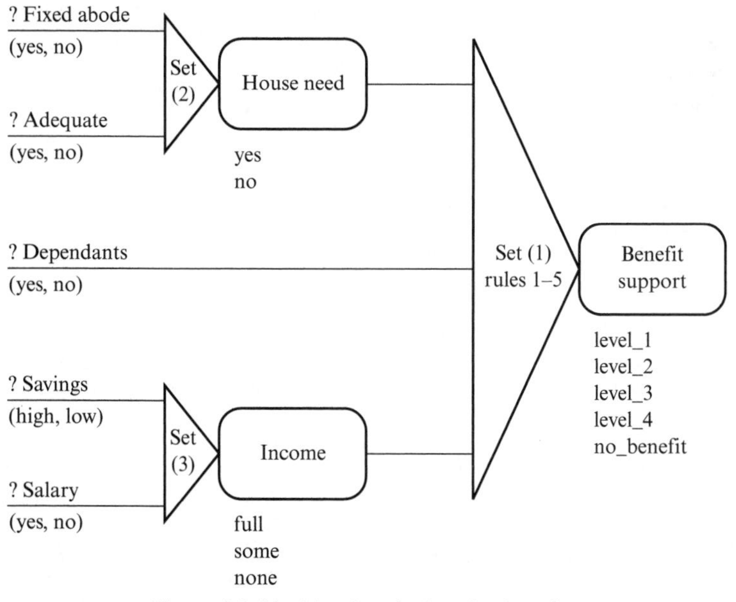

**Figure 9.3** Mockler chart for housing benefits

structing the decision table for the main decision and work backwards from top to bottom. Each decision table will generate a rule set, and each rule set should be numbered and written into the appropriate triangle on the Mockler chart (see Fig. 9.3). Before constructing each decision table, calculate the total number of rows required for the table. This can be found for rule set 1 as follows:

*Number of possible values that each condition takes:*

House need (yes, no) = 2

Dependants (yes, no) = 2

Income (full, part, none) = 3

**Therefore total rows = 2 × 3 × 2 = 12**

The complete decision table for the benefit is shown in Table 9.1. This shows 12 possible rows of combinations that could occur in the resulting table. When the number of rows is known, a table can be constructed by labelling each column with the name of the condition that will affect the final outcome (see Table 9.1). The first three columns in this table are house need, dependants and income. The last column in the table, benefit level, represents the outcome of this decision table and is dependent upon the values of the three condition columns. Each row in the table forms a rule relating the conditions to the outcome, or conclusion. For example, row A1 says that the benefit level is level_1, if the house_need is yes and the dependants is yes and the income is none. On the other hand, row A12 says that there will be no benefit payable to a claimant who has no house_need and has dependants and some income. The knowledge in each of these rows in the decision table will normally be provided by the domain expert.

Table 9.1 *Complete decision table for benefit main goal*

| *Rule* | *House need* | *Dependants* | *Income* | *Benefit level* |
|---|---|---|---|---|
| A1 | yes | yes | none | level_1 |
| A2 | yes | yes | some | level_2 |
| A3 | yes | no | some | level_4 |
| A4 | yes | no | none | level_3 |
| A5 | yes | yes | full | no_benefit |
| A6 | yes | no | full | no_benefit |
| A7 | no | yes | full | no_benefit |
| A8 | no | yes | full | no_benefit |
| A9 | no | yes | none | no_benefit |
| A10 | no | yes | none | no_benefit |
| A11 | no | yes | some | no_benefit |
| A12 | no | yes | some | no_benefit |

Table 9.2 *Reduced decision table*

| *Rule* | *House need* | *Dependants* | *Income* | *Benefit level* |
|---|---|---|---|---|
| B1 | yes | yes | none | level_1 |
| B2 | yes | yes | some | level_2 |
| B3 | yes | no | some | level_4 |
| B4 | yes | no | none | level_3 |
| B5 | yes | – | full | no_benefit |
| B6 | no | – | -- | no_benefit |

Decision Table 9.1 can be reduced, for it is clear that some conditions are meaningless in certain contexts. For example, notice that rows A7 to A12 can be reduced to a single row (shown in the reduced Table 9.2). This is because, if the house_need value in column 2 is no, then the recommended support for the claimant will always be no_benefit irrespective of what values the other factors take. Similarly, A5 and A6 can be reduced to B5 etc. This leads to the reduced Table 9.2.

### *Writing rules for the knowledge base (VP-Expert)*

Most rule-based expert system shells (including VP-Expert) represent knowledge by using *if... then* rules. This means that a rule begins with the keyword *if* followed by the conditions evaluated. Conditions can be linked by *and/or* logical operators. To convert the rows from the reduced decision table into rules, simply take each row and convert into *if...then* format by using the *and/or* operators as shown in Fig. 9.4. Insert keyword *if* before the first column condition in the table; link the other conditions using the *and* operator; and insert keyword *then* before the conclusion variable value. The rules for the reduced set of rows in Table 9.2 would be encoded as shown in Fig. 9.4 (called rule set 1). Note that there is not always a direct one-to-one correspondence between the rows in the table and the rules generated in Fig. 9.4, because rows B5 and B6 have been reduced to a single rule using the OR operator for this particular table. The reason for this is:

B5 gives *if* house_need = yes *and* salary = full *then* support = no_benefit

B6 gives *if* house_need = no *then* support = no_benefit

These two rules combined using the OR operator give:

*if* salary = full
    *or* house_need = no
*then* support = no_benefit;

```
RULE 1
IF house_need = yes AND
        dependants = yes AND
        income = none
THEN support = level_1;         --- converted from row B1

RULE 2
IF house_need = yes AND
        dependants = yes AND
        income = some
THEN support = level_2;         --- converted from row B2

RULE 3
IF house_need = yes AND
        dependants = no AND
        income = some
THEN support = level_4;         --- converted from row B3

RULE 4
IF house_need = yes AND
        dependants = no AND
        income = none
THEN support = level_3;         --- converted from row B4

RULE 5
IF house_need = no OR
        income = full
THEN support = no_benefit;      --- converted from rows B5 and B6
```

**Figure 9.4** Rule set 1 – main goal rules

The process is repeated for the next triangle in the Mockler chart to give rule set 2 as shown in Fig. 9.5.

```
RULE 6
IF fixed_abode = yes AND
        adequate = yes
THEN house_need = no;

RULE 7
IF fixed_abode = yes AND
        adequate = no
THEN house_need = yes;

RULE 8
IF fixed_abode = no
THEN house_need = yes;
```

**Figure 9.5** Rule set 2 – house need

Finally, the process is repeated for the third triangle in the Mockler chart to give rule set 3 as shown in Fig. 9.6.

**RULE 9**
IF salary = no AND
 savings = low
THEN income = none

**RULE 10**
IF salary = no AND
 savings = high
THEN income = some;

**RULE 11**
IF salary = yes
THEN income = full;

**Figure 9.6** Rule set 3 – income

### *Converting the rules into the target shell format – VP-Expert*

The rule sets generated are not in themselves enough to complete the adviser system because the goal has not been specified. That is, the expert system needs to know what it is supposed to do with the rules. Using the reserved word FIND does this in VP-Expert. The syntax for completing this task is "FIND support". This would instruct VP-Expert to FIND a value for support during the running of the program. Such a command is always positioned in the ACTIONS section of a VP-Expert program as described in the next section.

## 9.3 Structure of a VP-Expert program

In VP-Expert, a program is structured into three blocks. These are:

**1.** Actions
**2.** Rules
**3.** Questions

An action block sets the agenda for a consultation. It has to be the first block in a VP-Expert program and must begin with the keyword ACTIONS. Typical actions would involve a DISPLAY of some run-time header message, a directive to FIND some goal, and a directive to DISPLAY the value of this goal. Figure 9.7 shows an appropriate action section for the DHSS benefit expert system.

```
ACTIONS
        DISPLAY "welcome to the house benefits adviser system"
        FIND support
        DISPLAY "Recommended benefit: {support}."
;
```

**Figure 9.7** An action section for the DSS benefit expert system

A VP-Expert program must begin with the ACTIONS block, followed by the RULES block, and finally the QUESTIONS block. The questions to be asked in the VP-Expert program can be found by referring to the Mockler chart (Fig. 9.3). Since all variables on the left-hand side of the diagram are not dependent on anything else, they will therefore become questions to be answered by the end-user. Thus in the house benefit system, answers from the user will be required to questions for: fixed_abode, adequate, dependants, savings and salary. This follows from the fact that they do not connect back to any other dependency.

Figure 9.8 shows an appropriate question block for the DHSS benefit expert system. Note that the VP-Expert code syntax is to begin a question with the keyword ASK. The CHOICES clause that follows some of the questions is optional and would only be used with VP-Expert question syntax when the outcome of a question to the user is restricted to a selection from a menu list.

```
ASK fixed_abode: "Has the applicant a fixed abode or address?";
CHOICES fixed_abode: yes, no;

ASK adequate: "Has the applicant adequate accommodation?";
CHOICES adequate: yes, no;

ASK dependants: "Has the applicant any children or dependants?";
CHOICES dependants: yes, no;

ASK savings: "Has the applicant any savings ?";
CHOICES savings: high, low;

ASK salary: "Has the applicant a regular sufficient salary?";
CHOICES salary: yes, no;
```

**Figure 9.8** An appropriate question block for the DSS benefit expert system

The full VP-Expert program code listing follows in Fig. 9.9. The next chapter will explain the VP-Expert environment in a little more detail and include how to write the code using the built-in VP-Expert code.

```
/* Full VP-Expert listing for house benefit adviser system      */

/* Actions section    */

ACTIONS
        DISPLAY "welcome to the house benefits adviser system"
        FIND support
        DISPLAY "Recommended benefit: {support}."

;
/* Rule set 1    */
RULE 1
IF house_need = yes AND
        dependants = yes AND
        income = none
THEN support = level_1;

RULE 2
IF house_need = yes AND
        dependants = yes AND
        income = some
THEN support = level_2;

RULE 3
IF house_need = yes AND
        dependants = no AND
        income = some
THEN support = level_4;

RULE 4
IF house_need = yes AND
        dependants = no AND
        income = none
THEN support = level_3;

RULE 5
IF house_need = no OR
        income = full
THEN support = no_benefit;
```

**Figure 9.9** The full VP-Expert housing benefit program

```
/* Rule set 2 */

RULE 6
IF fixed_abode = yes AND
        adequate = yes
THEN house_need = no;

RULE 7
IF fixed_abode = yes AND
        adequate = no
THEN house_need = yes;

RULE 8
IF fixed_abode = no
THEN house_need = yes;

/* Rule set 3 */

RULE 9
IF salary = no AND
        savings = low
THEN income = none

RULE 10
IF salary = no AND
        savings = high
THEN income = some;

RULE 11
IF salary = yes
THEN income = full;

/* Questions section of listing */

ASK fixed_abode: "Has the applicant a fixed abode or address?";
CHOICES fixed_abode: yes, no;

ASK adequate: "Has the applicant adequate accommodation?";
CHOICES adequate: yes, no;

ASK dependants: "Has the applicant any children or dependants?";
CHOICES dependants: yes, no;
```

**Figure 9.9** The full VP-Expert housing benefit program (continued)

ASK savings: "Has the applicant any savings ?";
CHOICES savings: high, low;

ASK salary: "Has the applicant a regular sufficient salary?";
CHOICES salary: yes, no;

**Figure 9.9** The full VP-Expert housing benefit program (continued)

## Exercises

1. Amend the Mockler chart for the house benefit adviser so that the savings variable is changed from values none, some and full to correspond to numbers 0.0, 0.0 to 500, and above 500 respectively. That is, the user is expected to enter a number instead of the menu choices none, some and full, and the system will then deduce which category of savings to set.

2. The following is a decision table for the support level for operations in a private clinic. The operations are dependant on three factors whose values are shown in the table. Produce a reduced table, where possible, and write a rule set for this reduced table.

| *Rule* | *Member status* | *Reason* | *Problem* | *Concluding recommended support level* |
|---|---|---|---|---|
| **A1** | ok | new_case | serious | level_1 |
| **A2** | ok | new_case | non_serious | level_2 |
| **A3** | ok | follow_up | serious | level_1 |
| **A4** | ok | follow_up | non_serious | level_3 |
| **A5** | ok | info_other | serious | info_other |
| **A6** | ok | info_other | non_serious | info_other |
| **A7** | not_ok | new_case | serious | non_member |
| **A8** | not_ok | new_case | non_serious | non_member |
| **A9** | not_ok | follow_up | serious | non_member |
| **A10** | not_ok | follow_up | non_serious | non_member |
| **A11** | not_ok | info_other | serious | non_member |
| **A12** | not_ok | info_other | non_serious | non_member |

3. A large music store is considering developing an expert system for customer services. One task required by the system is dealing with customers who try to return faulty items. Clearly such items would not usually be accepted without a receipt. Another requirement is that goods will not be

accepted for credit if returned after 14 days without first being referred to the supervisor. A decision table has been completed with an expert as shown below.

| *Rule* | *Customer status* | *Goods status* | *Days since purchase* | *Action* |
|---|---|---|---|---|
| **A1** | important | good | <14 | accept |
| **A2** | important | fair | <14 | accept |
| **A3** | important | bad | <14 | refer |
| **A4** | important | good | >14 | accept |
| **A5** | important | fair | >14 | refer |
| **A6** | important | bad | >14 | reject |
| **A7** | unknown | good | <14 | accept |
| **A8** | unknown | fair | <14 | refer |
| **A9** | unknown | bad | <14 | reject |
| **A10** | unvalued | good | >14 | reject |
| **A11** | unvalued | fair | >14 | reject |
| **A12** | unvalued | bad | >14 | reject |

(a) From the tree diagram below, and the decision table above, produce a Mockler chart and then write the rule set ready for conversion to VP-Expert.

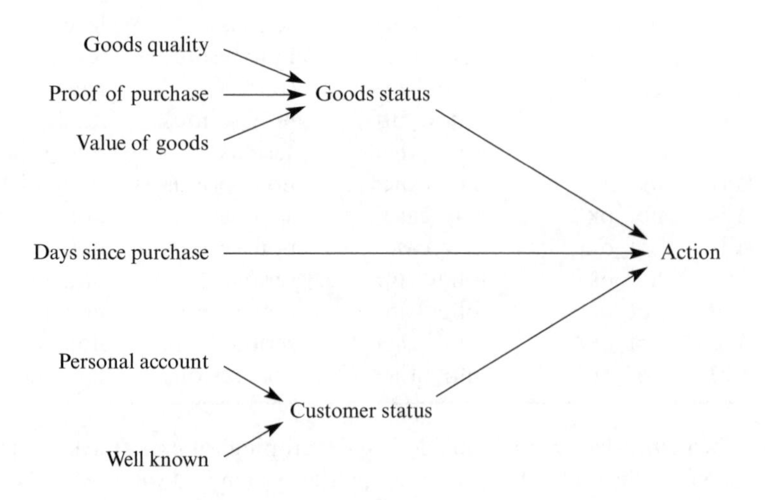

(b) Convert the following decision table to another rule set and extend the Mockler chart accordingly.

| *Goods quality* | *Proof of purchase* | *Value* | *Goods status* |
|---|---|---|---|
| damaged | ok | high | good |
| damaged | ok | low | fair |
| damaged | no | high | bad |
| undamaged | no | low | fair |
| damaged | no | low | bad |
| undamaged | ok | high | good |
| undamaged | ok | low | good |
| undamaged | no | high | bad |

(c) Convert the following decision table to another rule set and extend the Mockler chart accordingly.

| *Personal account* | *Well known* | *Customer status* |
|---|---|---|
| yes | yes | important |
| yes | no | unknown |
| no | yes | important |
| no | no | unimportant |

(d) Complete the expert system by writing a knowledge base in VP-Expert, and then include an appropriate action section along with a relevant questions section.

**4.** The following is a segment of a rule base that advises a house-bound married couple with children whether to go out, and where to go given certain data:

```
IF enough_money = yes
        AND baby_sitter = fair
        AND day = new_years_eve
THEN go_out = party;
```

```
IF enough_money = yes
        AND baby_sitter = good
        OR baby_sitter = fair
        AND day = Saturday
THEN go_out = cinema;

IF enough_money = yes
        AND baby_sitter = fair
        AND day = workday
THEN go_out = visit_friends;

IF enough_money = yes
        OR enough_money = no
        AND baby_sitter = poor
        AND day = workday
THEN go_out = no;

IF enough_money = no
THEN go_out = no;
```

(a) From the rules given above, write a decision table from the top-level rules, and identify any rules not included.

(b) Include an ACTIONS section for the rules above assuming backward chaining on the goal “go_out”. Trace the running of this system by listing the rule sequence fired and the facts deduced corresponding to the data given: enough_money = yes, baby_sitter = good, and day = Saturday.

(c) Trace the running of the system assuming forward-chaining inference on the data given below:

```
enough_money = yes,
baby_sitter = fair,
day = workday.
```

The following rules are added to the knowledge base:

```
/* Rule set 2 /*

IF applicant_age <14
THEN baby_sitter = poor;
```

```
IF applicant_age>16
        and experience = good
THEN baby_sitter = good;

IF applicant_age =15
        AND experience >2
THEN baby_sitter = fair;

IF applicant_age = 15
        AND experience <=2
THEN baby_sitter =poor;
```

(d) Draw a Mockler chart describing the whole system. Identify the questions, from the Mockler chart, and FIND the goal go_out by a full VP-Expert program. Run the program and check that it works by using the trace and explanation facilities within VP-Expert.

(e) An alternative approach to the design of the above system is to create a new variable called where_to_go, which takes the possible values cinema, visit_friends, party, etc. The go_out variable is redefined as taking the values yes or no. Explain what you think the benefits of this may be and modify the knowledge base to reflect this structure.

---

## *References and further reading*


Dologite, D. G. (1992) *Developing KBS using VP-Expert*, London: Macmillan.

Luce, J. (1992) *Using VP-Expert in Business*, New York: McGraw-Hill.

Mockler, R. J. (1993) *Developing KBS Using an Expert System Shell*, London: Macmillan.

Pigford, D. V. and Baur, G. (1995) Expert Systems for Business, 2nd edition, Danvers, MA: ITP.

CHAPTER 10

# Techniques using VP-Expert

**Objectives**

In this chapter you will learn:

- to know how to represent and use uncertainty in VP-Expert;
- to use facilities in VP-Expert to improve the user interface.

## 10.1 Representing and manipulating CFs in VP-Expert

VP-Expert supports the use of CFs, but not Bayesian inference, for handling uncertainty. CFs are also known as confidence factors in VP-Expert, and are represented on a scale from 0 to 100. This contrasts with MYCIN, which uses a scale from –1 to +1 to represent CFs.

### *Representing CFs in rule conclusions*

A CF can be represented in a VP-Expert rule as shown in the example below:

```
RULE 1.1
IF car_will_start = no
        THEN battery = faulty CF 65
```

RULE 1.1 shows the VP-Expert syntax for representing a CF in a rule conclusion. The rule indicates that the conclusion is true if the condition is true, but only with a CF of 65.

### *Representing CFs in questions*

A user can enter a CF to express the degree of confidence that the user may have in the correctness of a menu question. This will be entered during a con-

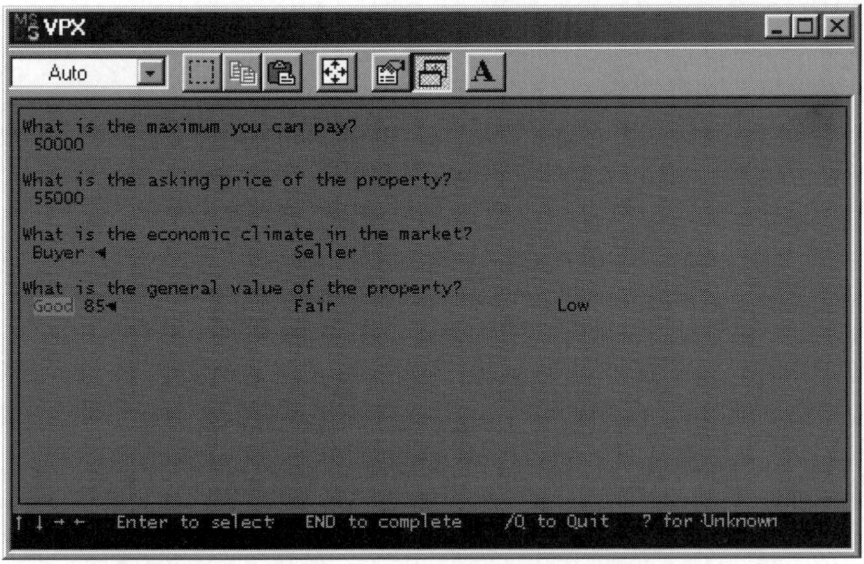

**Figure 10.1** Illustration of entering a CF associated with a question menu

sultation by highlighting the menu choice and pressing the <Home> key on the computer keyboard. A solid cursor will appear prompting the user to enter the numerical value corresponding to the belief in the value. To complete the selection, press the <Return> key on the keyboard. Figure 10.1 gives an illustration of how this would appear in VP-Expert. Notice that a CF of 85 has been entered by the user for the question: "What is the general value of the property?" This is a value that is associated with the menu choice "good".

### *Combining CFs in VP-Expert*

To combine CFs in VP-Expert, the rules are similar to those in MYCIN with a few minor differences.

### *Combining a condition CF with a conclusion CF*

To combine a condition CF with a conclusion CF, multiply the two CFs and divide by 100. That is:

Final CF = (CF condition × CF conclusion)/100

### Example

Find the final CF in the following rule:

RULE 1.2
IF engine_is_misfiring = yes CF 50
THEN replace_spark_plugs = yes CF 60

The final CF of this rule would be calculated using the following formula:

Final CF = CF condition × CF conclusion

Hence:

Final CF = 50 × 60/100 = 30 answer.

This answer conforms to intuition in the sense that if the condition leading to the conclusion is uncertain then the confidence in the conclusion will be less than it would have been if the condition was certain. If there is only 50% certainty in the condition then clearly this will reduce the confidence in the conclusion by 50%. That is, final CF = 30%.

### *Conjunction of several condition CFs*

To combine two or more CFs that are connected by AND conditions in a rule, take the minimum CF of all of the conditions.

### Example

Consider the following rule:

RULE 1.3
IF car is consuming excessive fuel CF 70
AND engine_is_misfiring = yes CF 55
THEN replace_spark_plugs = yes CF 50

RULE 1.3 has two AND conditions. To combine these two CFs the minimum of the two is 55. Hence, the CF of the conditions is 55. To find the final CF, combine this CF with the conclusion CF as in the last example. That is, multiply the two and divide by 100. Therefore:

Final CF = 55 × 50 /100 = 27.5 answer

### *Disjunction of several condition CFs*

To combine two or more CFs of conditions that are connected by OR statements, use the following formula:

$$CF\ (A\ OR\ B) = CF\ A + CF\ B - (CF\ A \times CF\ B/100) \tag{10.1}$$

where A and B represent two conditions.

#### Example

Consider the variation on the above rule:

```
RULE 1.4
IF car is consuming excessive fuel CF 70
    OR engine_is_misfiring = yes CF 40
        THEN replace_spark_plugs = yes CF 50
```

RULE 1.4 has two OR conditions. To combine these two CFs, the formula (10.1) above is used. This gives:

$$CF\ (A\ OR\ B) = 70 + 40 - (70 \times 40/100) = 82$$

Hence, as before, to find the final CF, combine this CF with the conclusion CF as in the last example. That is, multiply the two and divide by 100. This gives:

Final CF = $82 \times 50 / 100 =$ <u>41% answer</u>

## 10.2 The truth threshold

Another method of controlling uncertainty in a VP-Expert system is to use a *truth threshold* value. This is a number, in the range 0 to 100, that is supplied by the developer, to determine the minimum confidence factor required for a rule condition to be considered true. A threshold value is entered with a TRUTHTHRESH clause in the ACTIONS block or after the THEN part of a rule. If a value is not supplied, then VP-Expert uses an assumed default value of 20. As an example of how threshold values work, consider the following rule:

```
IF engine_is_misfiring = yes
    THEN replace_spark_plugs = yes TRUTHTHRESH = 50
```

Given the above rule, if the condition "engine was misfiring" was true with a CF of 45, then the rule conclusion "spark plugs are faulty" would fail since the CF assigned to the rule conclusion is going to be the same as the rule condition, which is 45; that is, less than the threshold value of 50.

## 10.3 Unknowns in VP-Expert

Besides working with uncertainty, experts sometimes have to deal with unknown information. For example, consider a medical expert who is asking a patient questions, in order to try and diagnose the patient's illness. If the expert were to ask the patient a question such as "did you have mumps when you were very young?", then, even if the patient answered the question with "I don't know?", the expert would still be expected to arrive at some conclusions, even if they were unknown. In the same way an expert system should be able to reason with unknown answers from questions to the user. If a user does not know the answer to a question, then VP-Expert allows the user to enter the question mark (?). However, VP-Expert can only handle this entry if the developer has included rules dealing with the appropriate variable and a keyword UNKNOWN. As an example of how unknown values for variables would be implemented in a VP-Expert program, consider the following rule:

```
IF engine_is_misfiring = UNKNOWN
        THEN spark_plugs = UNKNOWN;
        DISPLAY "Refer to car mechanic"
```

The above rule is interpreted as saying that if it is unknown that the engine is misfiring, then the condition of the spark plugs is unknown and the problem should be referred to the car mechanic.

## 10.4 Developing the user interface with VP-Expert

A range of commands can be used in VP-Expert to improve the quality of the user interface. This enables the builder to replace the default developer's interface with full-screen windows, instruction windows, colour selections, and so on. These commands would be entered in, or before, the ACTIONS section of the program. Some of the most commonly used are described below.

### *Creating a new Window – WOPEN*

A new window can be created for use during a VP-Expert consultation by using the WOPEN command. This command has the following syntax:

```
WOPEN A,B,C,D,E,F
```

A, B, C, D, E, F are called parameters, and take numerical values whose meanings are as follows:

| *Parameter* | *Purpose* |
|---|---|
| A | The number of the window being opened (between 1 and 9) |
| B, C | The row and column co-ordinates of the upper left-hand corner of the window |
| D | The number of rows the window should occupy (between 2 and 77) |
| E | The number of columns the window should occupy (between 2 and 77) |
| F | The colour of the background window (between 0 and 7) |

### *Activating a window – The ACTIVE command*

A newly created window can be activated (or displayed) using the ACTIVE command, followed by a single parameter (between 0 and 9). This is the number of the window in which the next used DISPLAY command will appear. Figure 10.2 illustrates the VP-Expert code that will display a window containing the text shown in Figure 10.3.

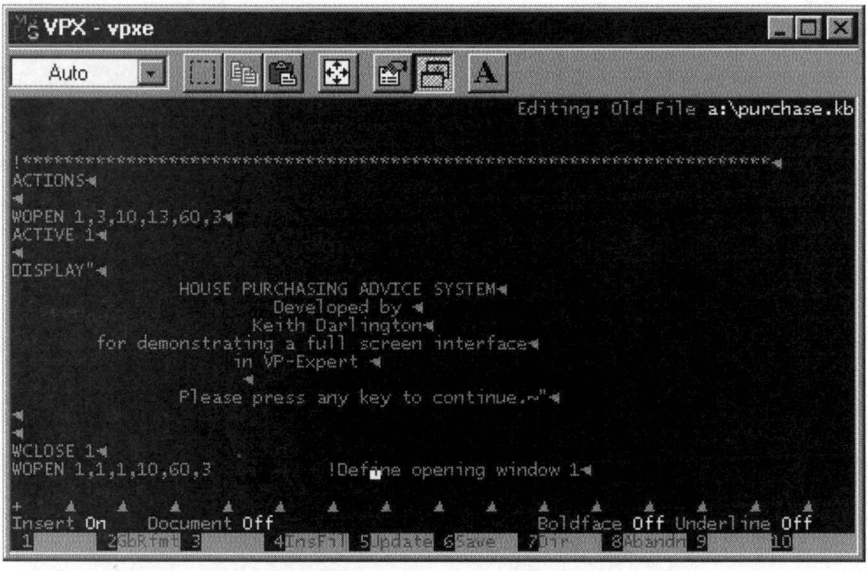

**Figure 10.2** VP-Expert code for displaying full-screen interface

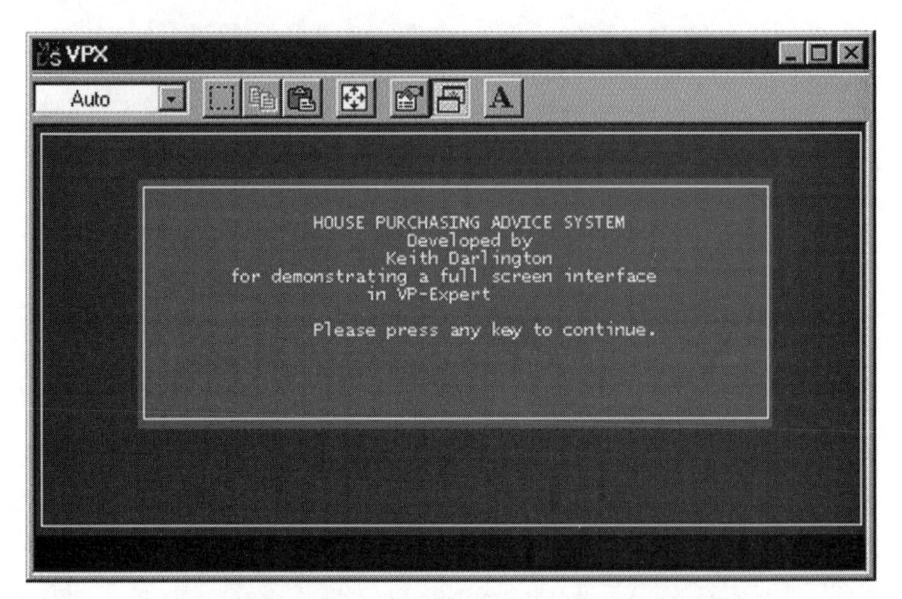


**Figure 10.3** Output resulting from Fig. 10.2 during run-time

The effect of the code shown in Fig. 10.2 will result in the output shown in Fig. 10.3 during run-time.

### *Specifying display co-ordinates – the LOCATE command*

It is possible to specify where in the ACTIVE window the next DISPLAY text should appear by using the LOCATE command. The LOCATE command uses two parameters to specify the row and column co-ordinates of where the DISPLAY text should begin to appear.

### *Closing a window – The WCLOSE command*

The WCLOSE command can be used to remove text windows that were created using the WOPEN command. This command uses one parameter (between 1 and 9) to specify the window number in a previously executed WOPEN command.

An example of the use of this command is shown in Fig. 10.4.

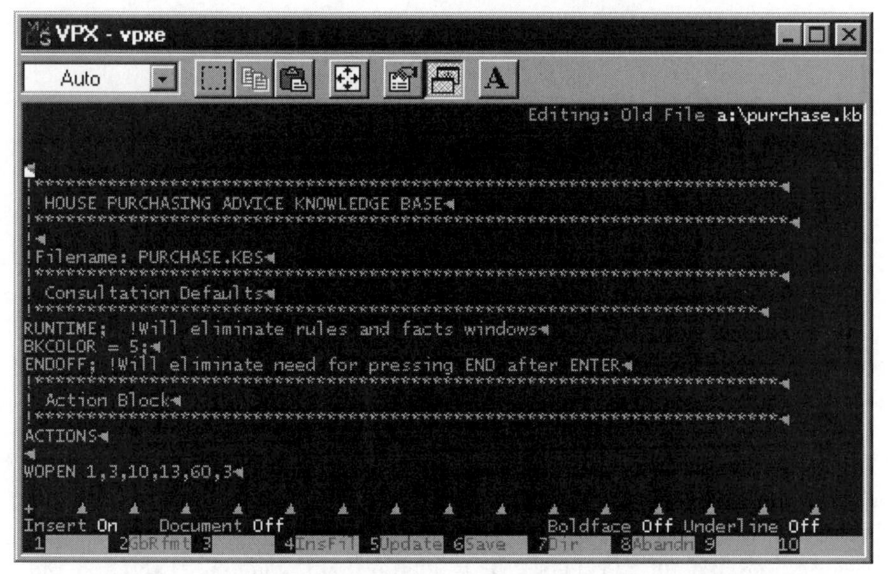


**Figure 10.4** Example of using run-time commands in a VP-Expert program

### *Controlling the VP-Expert run-time environment*

Another aspect of user interface control is the *run-time environment*. To enable a program to run in VP-Expert, the user has to select the consult option from the main menu. However, this tedious process can be bypassed by placing the command "EXECUTE" before the start of the ACTIONS section of a program. This means the selected file will run without having to enter the consult option (see Figure 10.4). Notice that another command called RUNTIME has also been used before the action block. This command is used to eliminate the facts and rules windows during run-time (see the Appendix).

## Exercises

**1.** Given the following rule, calculate the final CF.

```
IF   A CF 75 AND
     B CF 80 OR
     C CF 70
THEN D CF 60
```

**2.** Consider the following rules:

RULE 1.5
IF baby_sitter = good
AND enough_money = yes
THEN go_out = yes CF 90

RULE 1.6
IF baby_sitter = fair
AND enough_money = yes
THEN go_out = yes CF 60

RULE 1.7
IF baby_sitter = fair
AND enough_money = no
THEN go_out = no CF 90

Assume that TRUTHTHRESH = 40 and that the goal is "FIND go_out". What value will be assigned to go_out, and what is the final confidence in the conclusion in each of the situations in Table 10.1?

Table 10.1

| *Value of baby_sitter and CF* | *Value of enough_money and CF* | *Value assigned to go_out* | *Final CF of go_out* |
|---|---|---|---|
| Good, 75 | yes, 95 | | |
| Good, 60 | yes, 55 | | |
| Fair, 80 | yes, 70 | | |
| Fair | no, 25 | | |
| Fair | yes, 40 | | |

**3.** Are there any inconsistencies in the final conclusions in Table 10.1? Explain.

**4.** The following rule is taken from a forensic expert system. Find the final CF in the rule conclusion.

RULE 1
IF suspect_alibi = yes CF 60
AND suspect_DNA_sample = no CF 96
THEN suspect_not_guilty = no CF 90

**5.** Write down the VP-Expert command that will enable a knowledge base file to run without having to select the consult option.

**6.** A company which specialises in supplying business customers with second-user office equipment has approached you. Such equipment can vary in functionality and cost. Only one highly knowledgeable expert in this domain is now working with the company and this expert has expressed intentions to seek employment overseas in the near future. For this reason, senior management requires that this system is operational as soon as possible.

**(a)** Shown below is a dependency diagram for part of this advisory system.

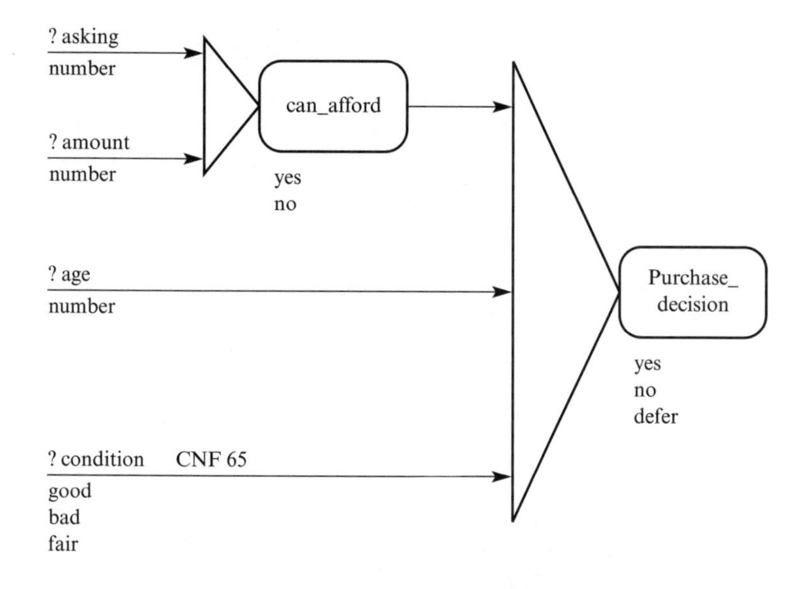


The purchase decision will only be *yes* if the customer is able to afford the equipment, and the age of the equipment is less than 3 years old, and the condition of the equipment is good. If the customer is able to afford the equipment, and the age of the equipment is less than 3 years old, and the condition of the equipment is fair, then the decision will be to *defer*. Any other combination will result in a *no* decision.

The customer will be able to afford the equipment only if the amount the customer has is greater than the price being asked for the equipment. Use the VP-Expert system shell to implement this system using rules. You should include questions the user would be required to answer when running the system and include a description of any inference action directives.

**(b)** If the user enters a CF with the answer to condition of 65 (see diagram above), how will that affect the CF of the final goal: that is, the purchase_decision?

### *References and further reading*

Dologite, D. G. (1992) *Developing KBS using VP-Expert*, London: Macmillan.
Luce, T. (1992) *Using VP-Expert in Business*, New York: McGraw-Hill.
Mockler, R. J. (1993) *Developing KBS Using an Expert System Shell*, London: Macmillan.
Pigford, D.V. and Baur, G. (1995) *Expert Systems for Business*, 2nd edition, Danvers, MA: ITP.

CHAPTER 11

# *The expert system development life-cycle*

**Objectives**

In this chapter you will learn:

- to compare and contrast the conventional system life-cycle with the expert system life-cycle;
- the stages undertaken during a typical expert system development;
- the predominance of prototyping in expert system development;
- to be aware of the methodologies for expert system development;
- to value the need for designing for maintenance of an expert system.

## 11.1 Introduction

Conventional software development is often viewed in terms of applicable life-cycle paradigms. This is because software development goes through a number of stages from initial conception to the finished product. For example, a commercial software company that is considering writing an accounts package would probably undertake a feasibility stage initially to see if the project is likely to be commercially viable. If the feasibility study has given the project a "green light" then the next stage may involve a detailed analysis of the problem; the stage following problem analysis might be the design of the new system, and so on.

As it happens, the approach in developing expert system software has some similarities with a conventional system. There are, however, some differences as indicated in Table 11.1. This table depicts a typical breakdown of the stages for both conventional and knowledge-based systems.

Despite many stages that appear to be similar, differences do emerge, particularly in the second phase. A number of methodologies have been adopted for expert system development. A methodology borrowed from conventional system development techniques is the stage-based approach.

Table 11.1 *Conventional and expert system life-cycle stages*

| *Conventional system* | *Knowledge-based system* |
|---|---|
| 1. Feasibility study | 1. Feasibility study |
| 2. System analysis | 2. Knowledge engineering |
| 3. Design | 3. Design |
| 4. Implementation | 4. Implementation |
| 5. Testing | 5. Testing |
| 6. Maintenance | 6. Maintenance |

## 11.2 The stage-based approach

As already stated, the essential difference between this and the conventional approach is in the knowledge engineering phase. System design, implementation and testing follow this phase. Thus, the stage-based approach treats development as a sequential process of completed stages, as shown in Fig. 11.1.

## 11.3 The prototyping approach

Conventional systems analysis is a well-defined activity in the sense that the details and duration of each task can be documented, monitored, managed and sustained if the project has been scheduled with adequate resources. Knowledge engineering is very different: for one thing, it is frequently difficult to specify, with clarity, the requirements in an expert system because of the abstract nature of knowledge. In expert systems, the end goals are typically not clearly defined. The goals are said to be "soft". This reflects the general difference between an expert system and a conventional system in that the former is concerned with the encapsulation, representation and manipulation of knowledge, which is often abstract in nature, while the latter focuses on the processing of data, which is clearly defined. Also, even if the requirements are specified completely, experts frequently have difficulty articulating their knowledge, so modifications to the knowledge base may be necessary. This means that the knowledge engineer will have to consult the expert again and agree to any modifications to the knowledge base. This iterative approach of development is by far the most successful paradigm used for expert system development; it is called *prototyping*. Note that the feedback loop, that is the number of stages, could vary between the knowledge engineering and the testing stage. In practice the prototyping stage will often involve the building of a *rapid prototype*. The idea is to provide a rapid springboard for discussion with users and experts and

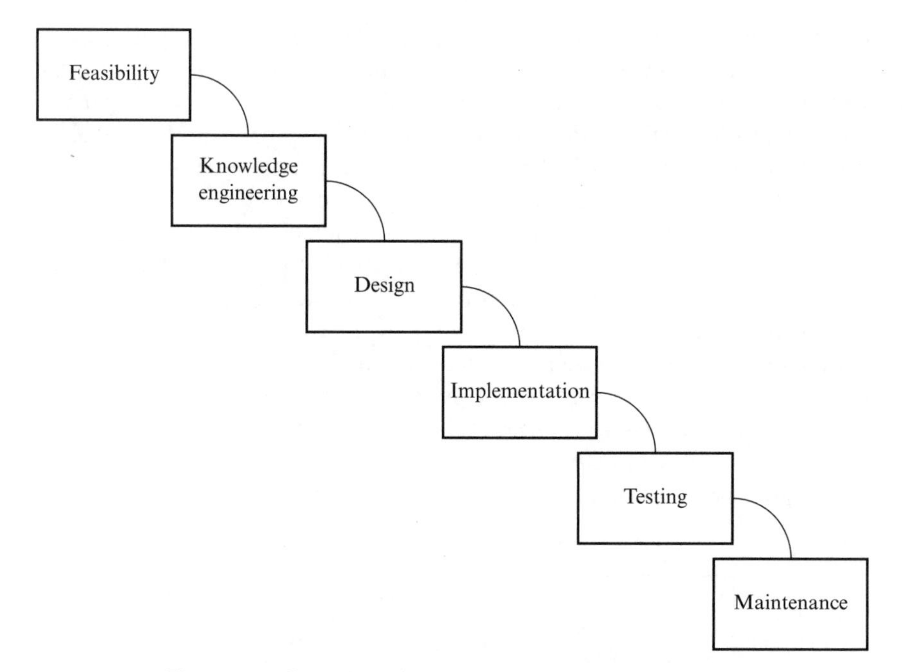


**Figure 11.1** Stage-based approach to system development

to demonstrate the system at an early stage to managers who may be sceptical about the use of expert system technology. Prototyping has been described as a "revolutionary change in the development process" (Naumann and Jenkins 1982) because it departs from the conventional software engineering approach. This prototype may be refined an unlimited number of times as a result of feedback and evaluation from users or experts. A prototyping approach has many other advantages, which are summarised below.

To understand how prototyping may work in practice consider first a conventional program development, for example a payroll system. The development of such a system would involve a set of inputs: namely, employee number, pay rate, overtime rate, hours worked, and so on. The outputs would typically be gross pay, tax paid, and so on. The processing would involve calculation of gross pay by multiplying hours worked by rate, and so on. Hence, the requirements for such a system can be clearly specified. A stage-based approach may be appropriate.

By contrast, consider a PAYE tax adviser expert system. What are the requirements? How much detail is necessary for the input data, and so on? To build this system would require identification of the problem, its domain, and its goals. This could involve a large system. But by using a prototyping approach, the developer might identify only one goal and a small part of the domain – perhaps 15% – as a starting point. The developer may just focus on one goal, perhaps income tax to be paid, and that part of the domain dealing with, for example, income tax for unmarried individuals. The developer would then perhaps code this knowledge in the form of a small set of rules perhaps using an expert system shell. The knowledge acquisition might involve deriving about 12 rules as a starting point for the first prototype.

The first prototype gives an indication of the likely look and feel of the end-product. It may well serve as a satisfactory basis for future development, in which case further refinements can proceed. Further refinements may involve adding manageable chunks to the existing prototype. This type of prototyping is called *incremental* prototyping since the remainder of the development will proceed with incremental advances on the first prototype. The iterative development life-cycle is shown in Fig. 11.2. The prototype may also turn out to be unsatisfactory, in which case it might be discarded. This type of prototyping is called *throwaway* prototyping.

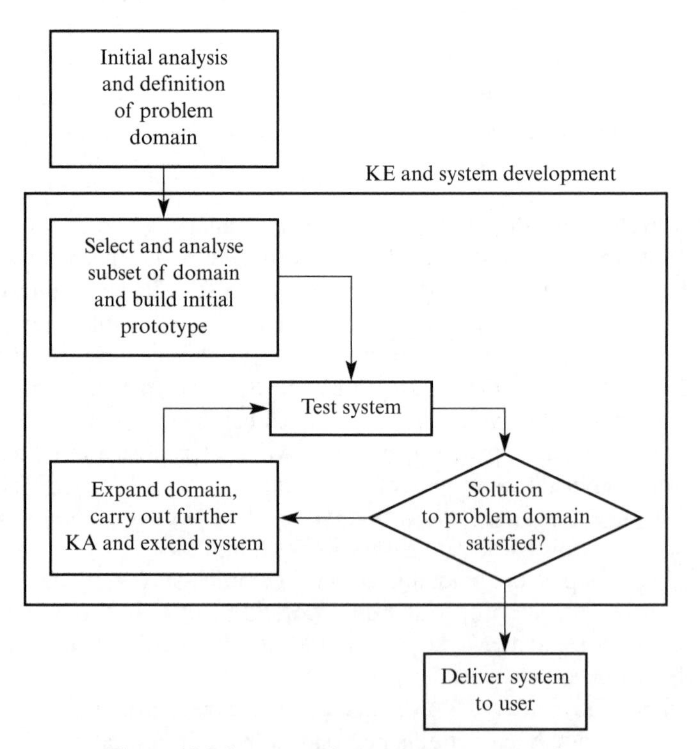


**Figure 11.2** Incremental expert system prototyping

### Self-assessment exercise

Some expert systems have failed because users have not been adequately consulted during the development process. How would you encourage the users of an expert system to become involved and inculcate enthusiasm for the project?

### *Advantages of rapid prototyping*

- It gives project developers a clear idea of whether it is feasible to attempt to tackle the complete application using expert system technology.
- It provides a useful product for discussion at an early stage.
- It can attract management or potential project sponsors with scope for quick demonstrations.
- It provides a means for experts to criticise the system or make amendments or exceptions to the rules.
- It helps sustain both the expert's and users' interests.
- It can also help to persuade any sceptical users involved in the system by encouraging an input during the refinement stages.
- It gives insight into the effectiveness of the intended tools to be used and the intended knowledge representation formalism, and provides scope to make such changes if necessary at an early stage.
- It may disclose unforeseen shortcomings in the proposed system that were unidentified during the feasibility stage.
- It might trigger suitability for expert systems in some related domain.

### Self-assessment exercise

Can you think of any disadvantages of rapid prototyping?

## 11.4 The feasibility study

The feasibility of an expert system has to be assessed against several criteria. However, a feasibility assessment strategy is necessary. One possible strategy, due to Beckman (1991), derives a list of issues and then assigns each issue a *weight* that reflects its relative importance. A score is then assigned to each issue. Table 11.2 shows, as an example, a partial list of issues that may be considered. The total sum of these weights is calculated and used to ascribe a percentage value to the likely success of the expert system project.

Table 11.2 *Feasibility-assessment issues*

| *Weight* | *Issue* | *Score* |
|---|---|---|
| 2 | Expert knowledge required | |
| 2 | Problem is well defined | |
| 1 | Problem requires uncertainty knowledge | |
| 2 | Problem domain is well documented | |
| 7 | FEASIBILITY % = TOTAL SCORE/TOTAL POINTS | |

The three main general criteria to consider in a feasibility study are:

**1.** Costs
**2.** Appropriateness
**3.** Availability of expertise

### *Costs*

A whole range of costs must be considered at the outset of an expert system development. Resources must be identified for analysis, design, coding, implementation and maintenance, in addition to hardware and software costs. Costs of sources of knowledge must also be known, as well as the likely time spent for user involvement during the design and analysis phases and for training in the use of the operational system.

### *Appropriateness*

As was seen in previous chapters, expert systems have been successful in problems that require a heuristic approach to problem solving. However, expert systems are not suitable for all types of problem. Indeed, experience has shown that not all heuristic problems are amenable to expert system solution. To determine those that that are amenable to expert system solution, the *telephone test* has turned out to be an effective measure. If a domain expert can solve the problem via a telephone conversation with the end-user, an expert system can probably be developed to solve the problem. The rationale underlying this test follows from the fact that the expert will have access to no additional information emanating from other sources, and the user will be able to describe the problem verbally. Conversely, if the user is unable to describe the problem verbally, or if the expert is unable, based on the telephone dialogue, to conclude a reasonable solution, then development of an expert system will be likely to fail. Ideally, for the telephone test to succeed, the time taken to solve the problem by a human expert should not exceed 30 minutes.

### *Availability of expertise*

Expert(s) must be identified for the domain, and must be available to devote sufficient time to the project. Moreover, the expert must be co-operative and enthusiastic, otherwise the project will have little chance of succeeding. When the project has been identified and authorised the process of knowledge engineering can begin.

## 11.5 The knowledge engineering stage

### *Purpose of system*

The knowledge engineering phase consists of a number of subphases. Clearly, the major purpose for developing the system must be established from the start. The purpose of the system must be identified. For example, it may be required to back up recommendations of an expert, or increase the quality and consistency of some task performed by the expert. It could even be to support novices in acquiring expertise in their domain of study. These are different tasks and will have different development requirements.

### *Domain and expert analysis*

Another aspect of the knowledge engineering phase is to identify the major concepts characterising the domain. The knowledge engineer will not necessarily be knowledgeable in the domain, and will therefore depend upon the expert to guide him or her through an understanding of the concepts. This stage is called *conceptualisation*.

## 11.6 Maintenance of expert systems

Few expert systems will remain static for very long. For instance, a taxation expert system is likely to require annual changes to reflect budget changes. Similarly, a printer manufacturer using an expert system help desk to assist customer problems would carry out updating as a result of the addition of new printers or removal of printers no longer supported by the company, and so on. Changes in company organisation, or political, economic or cultural changes, need updating if the expert systems are to remain effective. Yet many expert systems are not being maintained adequately. Feigenbaum (1993) believes that what he calls "knowledge rot" or lack of maintenance is one of the contributory factors impeding expert system acceptance.

The impetus for changes to an expert system can come from several sources. The expert, for example, may want to change the system to reflect changes in his or her knowledge about the domain. The user may also want to make changes, perhaps to modify the system to make rules work in a particular context, or make some other change to suit his or her own needs. Changes could also be necessary as a result of alteration in company procedure. Other changes may be necessary as a result of upgrading the operating system to a newer version. These will possibly mean changes in the dialogue itself, or changes to the interaction style, which could mean changes to the knowledge base. The knowledge engineer may, from time to time, need to make changes to link the system to external interfaces, such as databases, or to the rule base to eliminate redundant rules etc.

### *Designing for maintenance*

There are two main factors that will influence the maintainability of an expert system:

1. *Understandability*. If code can be easily understood it can be more easily maintained by maintenance engineers who were not members of the original development team.
2. *Changeability*. This is the ease with which the expert system can be extended and changes incorporated.

These two are related, but understandability is the most important. As far as program maintenance is concerned, many of the procedures practised in conventional software engineering should be adopted in developing the program code for an expert system. This usually means conforming to style guidelines such as consistent line spacing in program code, consistent indentation of lines of code, appropriate annotation, use of comments, correct use of upper and lower case characters, and so on. Moreover, code should be designed to facilitate modularity where possible. This will in itself make the maintenance task easier.

## Exercises

1. Discuss ways in which an expert system can be designed that will facilitate later system maintenance.
2. Outline the documentation that you think might be necessary for the completion of an expert system project.
3. Outline what the requirements are for the successful completion of an expert system project.
4. Discuss the major differences between the development effort of a conventional program and that of an expert system program.

**5.** A shoe manufacturer employs an expert in glues. The expertise involves knowledge of different types of materials, levels of stress in these materials, and the type of glue needed to reach that required level of stress. The expert is about to retire, and the manufacturer is keen to capture the expert's experience in an expert system that will operate on the shop floor, supporting decisions made by inexperienced staff, but will also act as a means of training. The expert has expressed willingness to co-operate. Although the company is very keen to use an expert system it has no experience of computerised systems but does understand that development might be slow and expensive. It is hoped eventually that the expert system will support an automated version of the process with very little human intervention.

Why would rapid prototyping be a good method of approaching the development of this system? Explain in detail what the process would involve and what platform you would use for the prototype.

---

## *References and further reading*

Beckman, T. J. (1991) Selecting expert system applications. *AI Expert,* February, pp. 42–48.

Browne, D. (1995) Ovum evaluates help desk tools. *Ovum Report.*

Feigenbaum, E. A. (1993) *Tiger in a cage*, Stanford Video Series.

Naumann, J. D. and Jenkins, A. M. (1982) Prototyping the new paradigm for systems development. *MIS Quarterly,* vol. 6, no. 3.

Preece, A.D. (1990) Towards a methodology for evaluating expert systems. *Expert Systems*, vol. 7, no. 4, 215–233.

Waterman, D. A. (1986) *A Guide to Expert Systems,* Reading, MA: Addison-Wesley.

CHAPTER 12

# Applications, the market and the future

**Objectives**

In this chapter you will learn:

- when to use expert systems;
- to recognise some of the most successful application areas of expert systems;
- to recognise some emerging application areas;
- to understand why company management has been reluctant to adopt expert systems;
- to identify likely trends in the future of expert systems.

## 12.1 Introduction

This final chapter in the book looks at the range of applications for which expert systems are suited, the current market in expert systems, and the applications likely to emerge in the future.

## 12.2 Applications of expert systems

Expert systems have found much use in industrial, commercial and financial application domains. Indeed, the range of expert system application areas is now so diverse that they have been successful almost wherever human decision support is involved. Most applications fall into the following task categories (Hayes-Roth, Waterman and Lenat 1933):

- *Diagnostic systems*. These infer system malfunctions from observable situations, for example medical, engineering and software diagnosis.
- *Planning and scheduling systems*. These are systems that design actions, for example automatic programming, robot movement, military strategy and even timetabling.

- *Interpretation systems.* These are systems that infer descriptions from observables, for example surveillance systems or speech understanding systems.
- *Prediction systems.* These are systems that infer consequences from given situations; examples are traffic prediction or weather forecasting.

The purpose of an expert system is not just to capture domain expertise, but to simulate a particular problem-solving task (or tasks) carried out within a domain. Table 12.1 illustrates working applications covering these tasks and other task categories that have not been included above.

---

## Self-assessment exercise

Credit and finance companies use expert systems for authorising customer loans. Can you list three or more possible benefits arising from using expert systems in this application domain?

---

## 12.3 Emerging applications of expert systems

Expert systems such as MYCIN, the medical expert system that diagnosed infectious diseases, and PROSPECTOR, an expert system for detecting mineral deposits, spawned a wave of other expert systems in the generic application areas of diagnostics and classification. Today new application areas are emerging that lend themselves well to expert systems. They include: knowledge publishing, help desk systems, Internet and World Wide Web tools, configuration and intelligent front-ends.

### *Knowledge publishing*

Knowledge publishing is a growing application area of expert systems. The idea of knowledge publishing is encapsulated in the concept of a book. A book is a passive object in that the onus is on the reader to find the passage of interest. Knowledge publishing delivers knowledge to the user actively by providing what the user specifically requested. There are examples in common use that are disguised: that is, working within other systems. End-users may be unaware that they are using an expert system. An example is Grammatik, the very popular grammar checker sold with WordPerfect software.

Table 12.1 *Expert system tasks and examples*

| *Expert system task* | *Description* | *Practical working systems* |
|---|---|---|
| Interpretation | Infer situation descriptions from sensor data | VATIA – advises auditors on VAT regulations |
| Planning | Design actions | DART – used by US government for planning transfer of soldiers and materials in the Gulf War |
| Diagnostics | Infer system malfunctions from observable data | MYCIN – used for diagnosing infectious diseases<br>TRACKER – used by BT for diagnosing a variety of faults in power supply equipment |
| Design | Configure objects under constraint | XCON – used by DEC to configure customer orders for VAX computers |
| Prediction | Infer likely consequences from situations or events | PROSPECTOR – a mineral exploration system that can compute probabilities of detecting minerals in various regions |
| Monitoring | Monitor system behaviour over time to guard against deviations that threaten stated goals | FRAUDWATCH – a system used by Barclays Bank to identify credit card fraud |
| Instruction | Diagnose and treat student misconceptions | GUIDON – a tutorial system for teaching the diagnostic problem-solving knowledge contained in MYCIN |
| Control | Diagnose, predict, repair and monitor system behaviour | VM – a system that monitors patients in an intensive care unit and controls the patients' treatments. The system characterises a patient's state from sensory data, identifies any alarms and suggests useful therapies |
| Repairing | Generate and administer remedies for system faults | TQMSTUNE – a system that tunes a mass spectrometer; that is, sets the instrument's operating controls to achieve optimum sensitivity |
| Debugging | Generate remedies for system faults | ONCOCIN – A system that helps treat cancer patients undergoing chemotherapy |

### Help desk applications

Help desk systems are likely to be a key growth area in the future and, according to Browne (1995), could be the saviour of expert systems. Most help desks have expert systems inside them, often CBR based, and growth in this market is predicted at 20% to 30% per annum. Large savings in time and costs can be achieved because people increasingly turn to the telephone when they have a problem rather than read manuals. The Compaq Computer company is a case in point. It now includes an on-line printer help desk with all printers sold. This program is called Quicksource. It includes 5000 cases of printer problems, and it is estimated that, consequently, 20% fewer customers are telephoning for support, resulting in substantial savings for the company as well as better service for its customers.

### Intelligent interfaces

Intelligent interfaces offer the potential to automate many tasks that could normally only be performed by a human user. Many computer users experience difficulty in accessing information required in computer systems. In an age of information overloading, users waste much time trying to find information; an example is the World Wide Web. One way to simplify this is to automate more of the interface process. Systems that filter, detect or explain information automatically offer the potential to give the computer more work and the user less (Lefley 1996). To be successful, these interfaces need to maximise efficiency and minimise mistakes.

### Expert systems and the World Wide Web

Intelligent interfacing covers a wide range of applications, and offers the potential of systems that deal with natural language, computer sound and vision, and automated reasoning. Intelligent agents can launch themselves without any distraction to the user or, indeed, without the user even being aware of their existence. Practical examples exist in a variety of areas but accessing information is a very common application area for intelligent interfaces. For example, the World Wide Web provides a massive worldwide library of information. However, the user can spend a great deal of time isolating the required information from this very large source. Expert systems have been developed to assist users in accessing large, specific databases on the Web. Typically, these expert systems would ask users the most relevant questions to elicit and identify the user problem. The expert system would then direct them to the information that offers the correct solution to the problem.

### *Configuration*

The configuration system XCON is one of the most well-known expert systems in use today (McDermott 1982). DEC built it for turning customer orders into feasible VAX computer configurations. The system was completed in the early 1980s. It has been an enormously successful application, with huge savings to the company and phenomenal benefits to the customer with order processing speed and accuracy levels impossible to achieve using manual methods. These benefits have already been described in Chapter 1. Another new wave of configuration applications is beginning to emerge suited to "mass customisation". One such example was developed by a Japanese company called Sekisui Heim. This company produces modular homes. Customer designs are produced and specifications sent to the company factory. At the factory, customer homes are made from a subset from an inventory of 300,000 parts. The system will decide a "picking plan". This system uses an inference method called *constraint-based reasoning*. One of the outstanding advantages of these configuration systems is the speeding-up of decisions, typically being reduced from several weeks to less than a day. Like so many such applications it is not only the performance speeds that have improved – the error rates have been reduced from an estimated 5% when manually operated to less than 1% as an expert system. The return on investment (ROI) for this system was estimated at less than 6 months despite taking over 3 years to develop.

### *Intelligent front-end processors*

An intelligent front-end (IFE) is software that sits between a user and a conventional software program. An IFE uses KBS or AI techniques to make more effective use of software packages. Classical examples are found in database software. An IFE would provide an easier-to-use interface with the database, for example by permitting more flexible user dialogue. The IFE would do this by gaining an understanding of the user's requirements, and then using this specification to generate instructions for running the software package. The dialogue with the user will often be interactive. The IFE may also use a variety of techniques, particularly when carrying out the dialogue with the user to produce a specification of the user problem. This idea has already been exploited in some commercial databases, such as Superbase.

### *Applications of expert systems on the Internet*

A great deal of expert systems research on the Internet has occurred in the last 5 years. For example, Far and Koono (1996) describe a Web-based distributed expert systems (Ex-W-Pert System) for sharing KBS and groupware development activities. The expert system development corporation EXSYS (illustrated

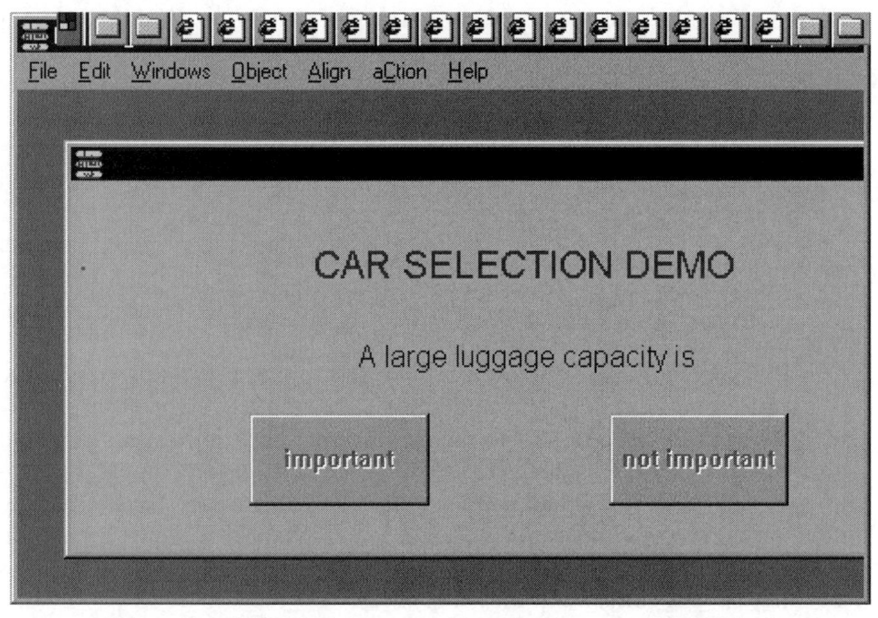


**Figure. 12.1** EXSYS Web Interactive Illustration (courtesy of EXSYS Inc.)

in Fig. 12.1) has also developed several interactive applications over the World Wide Web. Moreover, expert system techniques such as rule-based reasoning are being applied to a range of Internet tools, from the filters in an email reader to Internet search engines. Many companies are deploying CBR as well as rule-based technologies to make their Web sites smarter. For example, the CBR toolkits KATE-CBR and CBR-Works have interfaces that allow direct integration with Web servers. The companies can build customised search engines that invite customers to fill in a questionnaire based on a case base.

## 12.4 Reasons for some scepticism towards expert systems

There was a great deal of scepticism about expert systems in the 1980s. Not least amongst the reasons for this was the way that AI and expert systems were reported at the time. Exaggerated claims were made about AI and expert systems, so many people anticipated delivery of very powerful systems. When these systems failed to deliver what was expected, scepticism followed.

Another reason for the lack of acceptance of expert systems is the lack of quality knowledge acquisition tools and the consequent difficulty in obtaining knowledge. Much progress has already been made in this area in recent years, particularly with regard to automation of knowledge acquisition using machine learning in the form of induction engines, CBR, and so on.

Another problem for the acceptance of expert systems has been the lack of development standards in common use. Several standards have emerged in conventional software development. For example, the SSADM development cycle is now a standard; there is no such standard in expert system development. The effect is to leave computing managers sceptical. However, the situation is beginning to change with the emergence of a methodology for development called KADS (Knowledge Acquisition Design System). This is now becoming the *de facto* standard methodology for building expert systems (Tansley and Hayball 1993). However, KADS can be an expensive methodology. Its use therefore is more suited to medium-sized and large expert systems, and frequently cannot be justified for small expert systems.

Finally, there is, as Feigenbaum (1993) says, the problem of "knowledge rot". Many good systems that were developed in the 1980s seem to have faded into oblivion as a result of maintenance difficulties. Yet most systems will require maintenance for many reasons, such as changes in company procedures, government legal changes, etc. For example, an expert system in the finance domain would need at least annual maintenance to allow for taxation changes in the Budget. Maintenance may involve adding, deleting or perhaps amending existing rules in the knowledge base.

## 12.5 The future of expert systems

Despite the scepticism outlined in the previous section, the future looks bright for expert systems. As was seen in Section 12.3, many new application areas continue to surface. This interest has led to a demand for better knowledge engineering tools that enable less experienced builders to develop systems. Advances in computer hardware such as Pentium PCs have enabled expert systems to be built using a more sophisticated graphical user interface operating environment. Improvements in areas of expert system technology, such as knowledge representation, knowledge acquisition, development tools, expert system design, and the programming of expert systems, continue to be made.

### *User interface improvements*

Improvements in the quality of the user interface have been notable in recent years in both the content of the communication and the physical means of communication between the user and the expert system. In addition to high-quality graphical user interfaces, many expert systems provide capabilities for natural language interaction, speech recognition and high-quality explanations. Improvements in this area are likely to continue in the future.

### *Knowledge representation*

Various representation schemes were discussed in Chapter 3. Tools that enable the integration of these schemes will continue to improve in the future. This will enable the knowledge engineer to combine models of domain knowledge, which provide a more realistic representation of the domain. Research in new representation schemes will also continue. For example, a means of representing knowledge, called *model-based reasoning*, is now emerging.

### *Knowledge acquisition*

The knowledge acquisition stage of expert system development is well known for precipitating the so-called "bottleneck" phase. Manual methods of knowledge acquisition often require interviews and lengthy verbal analysis. This is time consuming and expensive. The process of automating knowledge acquisition is therefore an issue of extreme importance. Automated knowledge acquisition tools (Parsaye and Chignell 1988) vary in capabilities at present from generating rules from examples given by the expert (Hart 1989) to consistency checkers. Automated knowledge acquisition tools can decrease the costs of acquiring knowledge (Martin and Oxman 1988). They can decrease both the skills required and the time taken for the knowledge engineer to acquire the necessary knowledge.

## 12.6 Conclusions

The perception of the usefulness of expert systems was quite low in the 1980s. As already stated, AI and expert systems were excessively "hyped", leading to high expectations. When the AI community failed to deliver such systems, pessimism followed. As Robert Milne (1985) said:

> The serious user is not overselling AI, the casual user is. I have heard many briefings of "blue sky" applications of expert systems. These people do not really understand AI so they dream up something wonderful that can never be built. As a result of the idea being "sexy", much effort and publicity surrounds it. Eventually this project will fail and more people will stop believing in the potential for AI. This is bad for several reasons. First, AI got a bad name, when it was some researcher or project leader that didn't know what they were doing. Secondly, a good chance for a successful application has been missed.

Much has changed since the above view was expressed. In the 1980s expert systems were predominantly standalone programs, as exemplified by XCON, but in the 1990s they are frequently found lurking within other systems, in the form of intelligent front-ends to other programs, or supporting intelligent searches on the World Wide Web, or carrying out a variety of other tasks that were not anticipated in the 1980s.

Many businesses experimented with expert systems in the 1980s without a clear understanding of their limitations; consequently many expert systems ended up gathering dust on the shelf. The lesson now being learned is that expert systems still have much potential in business today, but it is important to gain a clear understanding of the limitations of the technology first.

## Exercises

1. Expert systems are routinely developed over very narrow domains. Why was narrowness crucial to the practical success of early approaches to building expert systems?
2. The first generations of rule-based expert systems were said to be "brittle" in the sense that they were unable to respond to variations in input data and problems. Give an example of how this might happen in a medical expert system like MYCIN, and explain how expert systems could be made less "brittle".
3. Take an instance of a skill that is likely to be suited to a rule-based expert system, such as choosing a university to study for a particular course, or completing a job application form. Try to represent some knowledge in this system by formulating some rules.
4. There are many free demonstrations of expert system software. Find three on the Web and download them. Evaluate them and report your findings.

### *References and further reading*

Browne, D. (1995) OVUM Report, UK.

Far, B.H and Koono, Z. (1996) Ex-W-Pert System: a Web based distributed expert system for groupware design. *Expert Systems with Applications,* vol. 11, no. 4.

Feigenbaum, E. A. (1980) KE the applied side of AI. Report STAN-CS-80-812, Dept. of Computer Science, Stanford University.

Feigenbaum, E. A. (1993) *Tiger in a Cage*, Stanford Video Series.

Hart, A. (1989) *Knowledge Acquisition for Expert Systems,* New York: McGraw-Hill.

Hayes-Roth, F., Waterman, D. A. and Lenat, D. B. (1983) *Building Expert Systems,* Reading, MA: Addison-Wesley.

Lefley, M. (1996) Intelligent interfacing. *ISIP News,* DTI.

Martin, J. and Oxman, S. (1988) *Building Expert Systems: A Tutorial,* Hemel Hempstead: Prentice Hall.

McDermott, J. (1982) R1: a rule based configurer of computer systems. *Artificial Intelligence,* vol. 19, no. 1.

Milne, R. (1985) *IEEE Symposium on Expert Systems in Government,* pp. 66–67.

Parsaye, K. and Chignell, M. (1988) *Expert Systems for Experts,* New York: John Wiley.

Tansley, D. S. W. and Hayball, C. C. (1993) *Knowledge Based Systems Analysis and Design (A KADS handbook),* BCS Practitioner Series.

Waterman, D. A. (1986) *A Guide to Expert Systems*, Reading, MA: Addison-Wesley.

# Appendix

## A.1 Using the VP-Expert environment

The VP-Expert system is an expert system shell that can run on a PC using Windows 98 or DOS. When the VP-Expert program is run, the main menu screen will appear as shown in Fig. A.1:

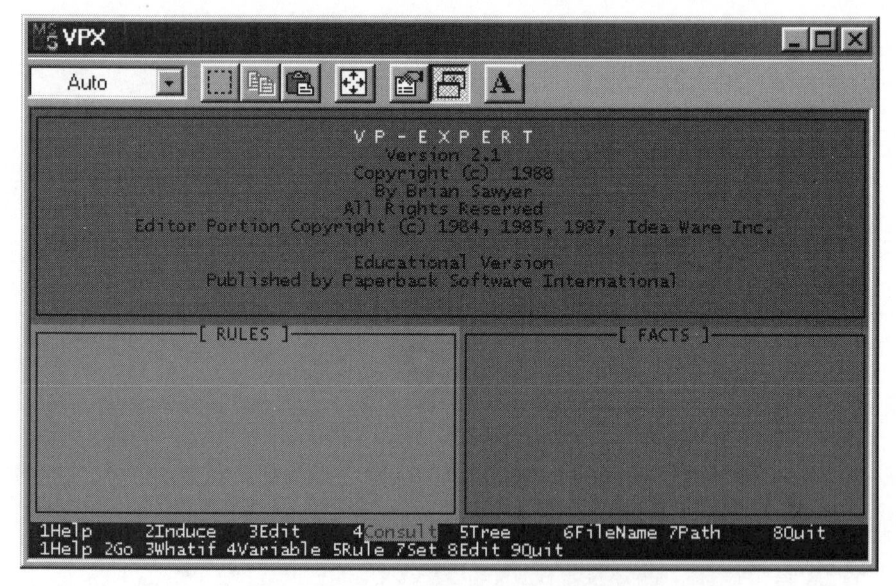


**Figure A.1** Main menu screen in VP-Expert

The figure shows how the screen is partitioned into three windows. The default colour for the top window is green, the lower left-hand side window's default colour is light blue, and the right-hand side lower window's default colour is white. A number of main menu options are available for selection.

## A.2 Loading or saving knowledge base files

If it is intended to load a previously saved file, then choose option 6, FileName, from the main menu and press <Return>. The window as shown in Fig. A.2 appears with a file list similar to that as shown. A selection can be made as usual with the cursor keys to highlight and <Return>.

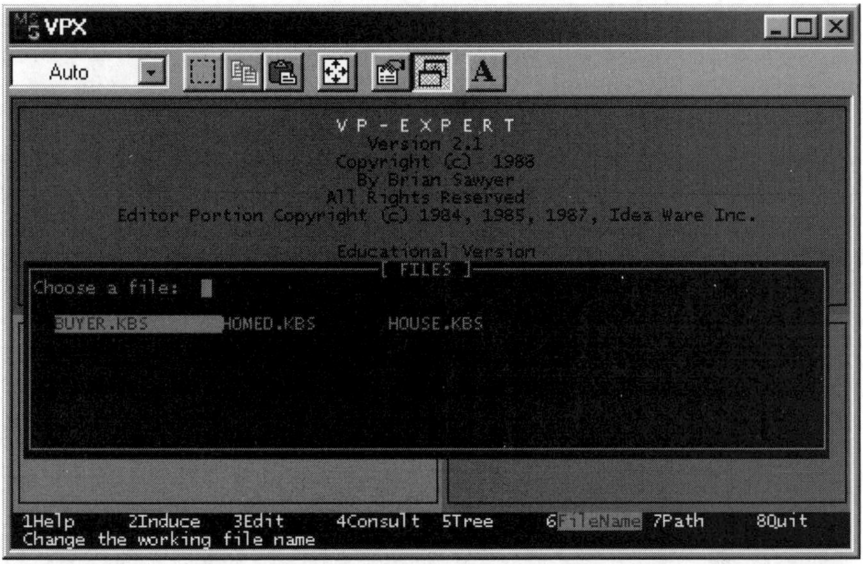

**Figure A. 2** Loading a knowledge base in VP-Expert

## A.3 Changing the path in VP-Expert

Sometimes, it may be necessary to load or save knowledge base files to a floppy disk instead of the default drive, that is the hard disk. To save files on the floppy disk, it will be necessary to change the path from the default drive C to the A drive. To do this, choose the option from the menu options path on the main menu screen. A dark-blue-coloured window as shown in Fig. A.3 will appear on the main screen.

Type a: <Return>.

When a file has been selected, it is loaded into main memory and can be modified using the Edit option, or it can be executed using the Go option.

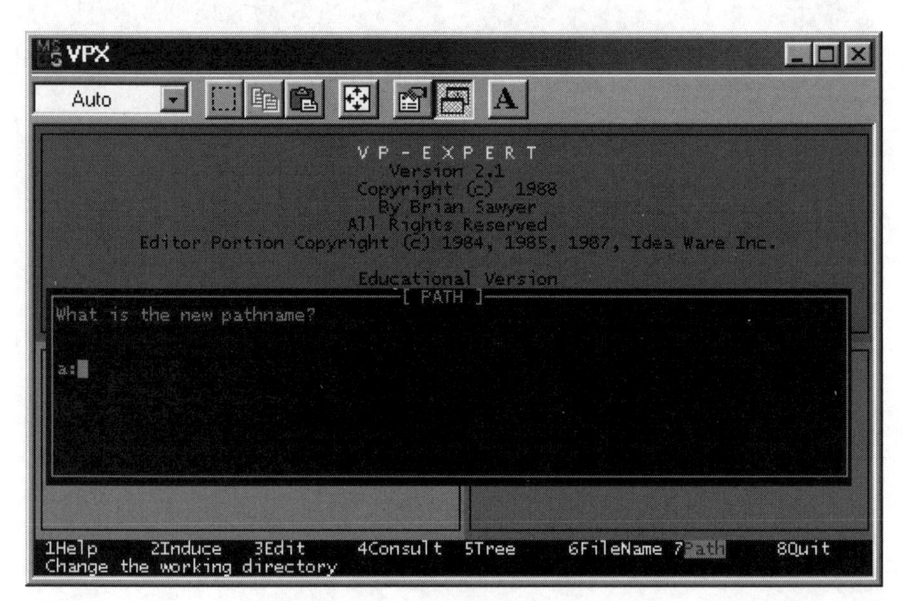


**Figure A.3** Changing the drive path in VP-Expert

## A.4 Running an existing expert system

To run an existing expert system, select a file from the list as shown in Fig. A.2 previously. Then select menu option Consult. Thus, if the file called Buyer is selected from the list of files as shown in Fig. A.2, then Buyer has been loaded into main memory and can now be executed. Figure A.4 shows the first screen that is displayed during execution of this knowledge base.

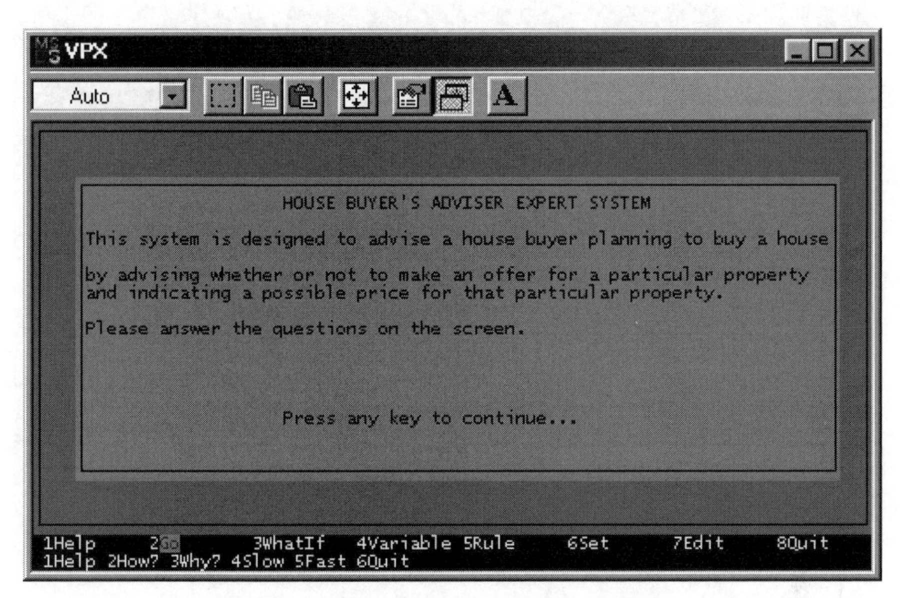


**Figure A.4** Executing a knowledge base file

## A.5 Editing an existing knowledge base file

The VP-Expert code can be examined by using the built-in VP-Expert editor. To use the editor, select the Edit option on the main menu at the bottom of the screen (see Fig. A.5). The code shown in Fig. A.5 is that taken from the knowledge base file that has been loaded, called Buyer.

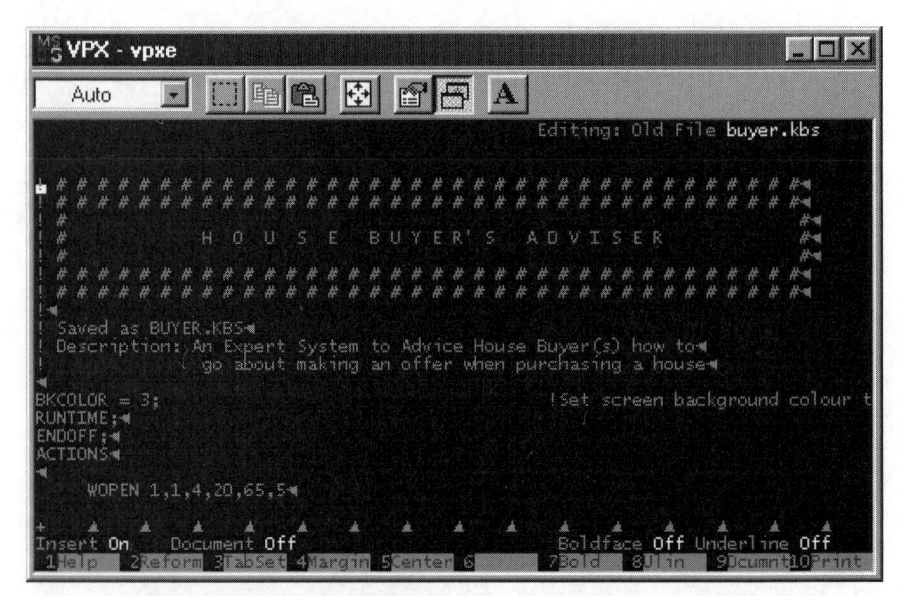


**Figure A.5** Using the Edit option to view a knowledge base file

## A.6 Creating a new VP-Expert knowledge base

To create a new file in VP-Expert, select the FileName option from the main menu as shown in Fig. A.2. A list of files will appear giving possible choices. To begin building a new system, ignore the file list and type the intended new name of the file (maximum eight characters) instead of using the cursor keys to select from the given list. When the new filename is typed, select the Edit option from the main menu. A screen will appear consisting of white text against a black background. The source code for a VP-Expert can now be entered and VP-Expert will automatically assign a kbs extension to this file. For example, Fig. A.6 is the edit screen for entering a new file called house2. The ACTIONS block, RULES block and QUESTIONS block that were discussed in Chapters 9 and 10 can now be entered. When finished press the ALT and F6 keys to save the file and return to the main menu.

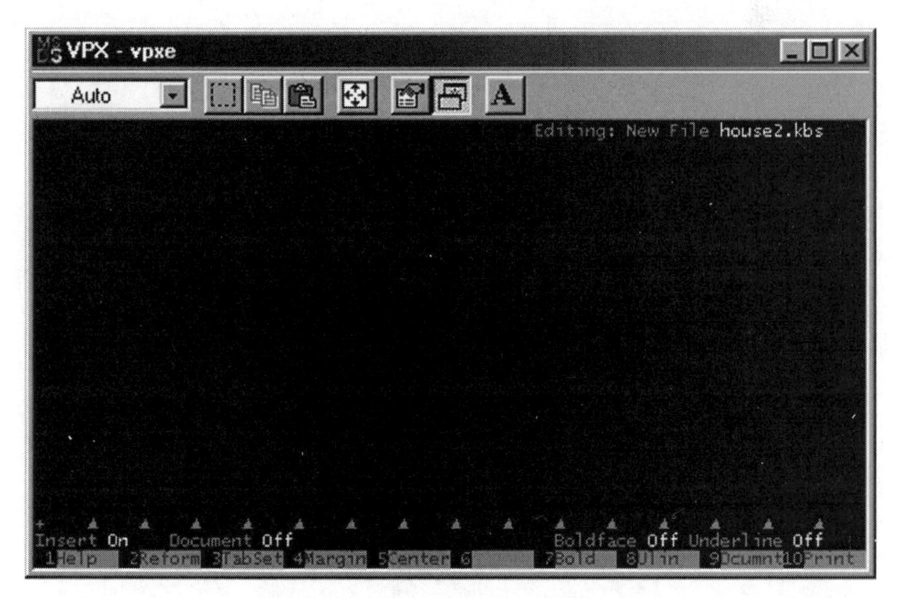


**Figure A.6** Editing a new knowledge base

# Index